CITIZENS OF HEAVEN

RESIDENTS OF EARTH

Lindsey Garmon

ISBN: 978-0-89098-547-2

Cover design by Jonathan Edelhuber

TABLE OF CONTENTS

Introduction

Christians! Understand and Claim Your Identity!

As followers of Jesus, do we really know and understand who and whose we are?

Five significant words in our English Bibles capture the heart and core of every Christian's primary identity. Paul wrote these gripping words to believers who lived in the city of Philippi in the first century. Even though they were caught up in the daily activities of life and the typical responsibilities related to citizenship on this earth, Paul made this amazing assertion in Philippians 3:20:

Our citizenship is in heaven.

Your Primary Citizenship—Where Is It?

How do you answer that question?

In view of Paul's words in Philippians 3:20, where is your primary citizenship—is it on earth or in heaven?

When you hear the word "citizenship," what immediately comes to your mind? Does this word prompt you to think about connections that you have on this earth, or does the word trigger thoughts of your spiritual link to a heavenly homeland? The goal of this book is to so thoroughly explore the benefits and responsibilities of heavenly citizenship that the very mention of citizenship will immediately rivet your mind first and foremost on your ties to heaven, rather than your connections to earth.

From time to time, we are required to complete official documents that ask for our "country of citizenship." When filling out such papers, has it ever been your first inclination to write in the word "heaven"? As you are in the process of supplying answers to these questions, have you ever had to suddenly remind yourself that these documents are asking for information pertaining to your earthly status rather than your heavenly ties? Can you imagine being so focused on the significance of your heavenly citizenship that your earthly connections pale in comparison? When the issue of citizenship arises, what immediately comes to your mind?

The more we study the implications of heavenly citizenship and learn to see the realities of our lives through eyes of faith, the more the unseen world will begin to appear in greater clarity. And, as our spiritual vision improves, the significance of our heavenly citizenship will gradually rise to a level that overshadows our earthly ties and connections—as important as they are.

The Bible Declares Our Heavenly Citizenship

The testimony of the Bible clearly indicates that, even though we are living as temporary residents of earth, our primary citizenship is in heaven. In numerous places, the message comes through loud and clear.

Look again at Paul's words in Philippians 3:20. His point is amplified when you compare the wording of this verse in different translations of the Bible. Note the interesting variations.

> But our citizenship is in heaven. And we eagerly await a Savior from there, the Lord Jesus Christ (NIV).

> But we are citizens of heaven, where the Lord Jesus Christ lives. And we are eagerly waiting for him to return as our Savior (NLT).

> But our homeland is in heaven, and we are waiting for our Savior, the Lord Jesus Christ, to come from heaven (NCV).

> But we are a colony of heaven, and we wait for the Savior, who comes from heaven, the Lord Jesus Christ (Moffatt "1913").

This idea that Christians are "citizens of heaven" aligns with the prayer that Jesus offered for His disciples just prior to His ascension. Speaking to His Father, Jesus said

> I have given them your word and the world has hated them, for they are not of the world any more than I am of the world. My prayer is not that you take them out of the world but that you protect them from the evil one. They are not of the world, even as I am not of it. Sanctify them by the truth; your word is truth (John 17:14-17).

Other biblical references reinforce the idea that as citizens of heaven, Christians live on earth as strangers, pilgrims, and sojourners—outsiders.

> Jesus said, "My kingdom is not of this world. If it were, my servants would fight to prevent my arrest by the Jews. But now my Kingdom is from another place" (John 18:36).

All these people were still living by faith when they died. They did not receive the things promised; they only saw them and welcomed them from a distance. And they admitted that they were aliens and strangers on earth. People who say such things show that they are looking for a country of their own. If they had been thinking of the country they had left, they would have had opportunity to return. Instead, they were longing for a better country—a heavenly one. Therefore God is not ashamed to be called their God, for he has prepared a city for them (Hebrews 11:13-16).

Since you call on a Father who judges each man's work impartially, live your lives as strangers here in reverent fear (1 Peter 1:17).

Dear friends, I urge you, as aliens and strangers in the world, to abstain from sinful desires, which war against your soul. Live such good lives among the pagans that, though they accuse you of doing wrong, they may see your good deeds and glorify God on the day he visits us (1 Peter 2:11, 12).

Our Songs Declare That We Are Strangers on Earth

What about the wording in some of the great Christian hymns we love to sing? What do these songs say about our heavenly citizenship and the demanding journey that we are presently making through this foreign territory that we call earth?

Frequently, as we sing songs about heaven, powerful messages come through the lyrics. Are we paying attention? The messages are quite revealing—maybe even shocking to some. For example, we sing with great joy, "This world is not my home; I'm just a passing thru...And I can't feel at home in this world any more!" Do those words resonate with you? With deep feeling and confident expectation, we declare in song that, in this world, we are straying pilgrims in route to a forever home, which is just beyond the rolling river of death. There really are powerful messages in our great songs of faith. As a Christian pilgrim, sing! Sing out with great confidence and faith as you make your way toward home. Try it and you will discover that the messages of our songs will give you added strength and endurance for the long haul.

Do We Understand and Own Our Heavenly Citizenship?

We've read these Bible verses and others like them numerous times. We have sung these songs and others like them again and again. Yet, many of us have never really understood or owned our spiritual identity as resident-aliens in this world. We've driven our stakes too deeply in earthly soil. We have traveled too heavily—loaded down with the stuff of this foreign country. We have become comfortable and cozy. As someone put it, "We are prepared to go to heaven—just not ready." We've adjusted to the good life in this world. Like foreigners who come to America and don't want to go home, we have lost our deep love and longing for the homeland of heaven. Could it be that we need to get refocused on our primary citizenship?

How Are We to Live As Citizens of Heaven While Sojourning As Residents of Earth?

Living in this world as foreigners, strangers, and pilgrims is a common theme in both the Old and New Testaments. Thus, the Bible becomes our "Immigration Manual," informing us about the few years we spend as foreigners in this present world. We look to the Scriptures as our dependable and practical guide for understanding how our heavenly citizenship should affect our daily behavior during this earthly residency.

Too many of us are living without a keen awareness of and appreciation for our heavenly citizenship—and all that it means. The appetites and attractions of this present world have a powerful way of blurring our vision of spiritual reality. Could we be living in a state of spiritual amnesia? Do we really understand and value our status as citizens of heaven? Do we grasp and accept the responsibility that this brings?

How we need to rediscover the exciting and life-changing fact of our heavenly citizenship! Though we live on this earth, we are members of the colony of heaven. We must learn how to effectively live "in the world," while not being "of the world," yet faithfully carrying out our God-given mission "to the world."

CHAPTER 1

The Meaning and Means of Heavenly Citizenship

Christians Hold Primary and Secondary Citizenships

As believers in Christ, we live simultaneously in two spheres. First and foremost, we live as citizens of heaven and consider this high calling as our primary and permanent citizenship. Our deepest loyalty will always be to the land of our "new birth"—heaven.

> Everyone must submit himself to the governing authorities, for there is no authority except that which God has established. The authorities that exist have been established by God. Consequently, he who rebels against the authority is rebelling against what God has instituted, and those who do so will bring judgment on themselves (Romans 13:1, 2).

> For the grace of God that brings salvation has appeared to all men. It teaches us to say "No" to ungodliness and worldly passions, and to live self-controlled, upright and godly lives in this present age, while we wait for the blessed hope—the glorious appearing of our great God and Savior, Jesus Christ (Titus 2:11-13).

> Peter and the other apostles replied: "We must obey God rather than men!" (Acts 5:29).

Our situation is similar to that of Paul, the apostle. In a first-century setting, he boldly exercised his Roman citizenship and frequently took advantage of his rights as an earthly citizen (Acts 16:37-40; 22:22-29). Yet first and foremost, Paul understood that, as a follower of Jesus Christ, he was "a citizen of heaven."

Understanding the Historical Context of Philippians 3:20

Because this five-word assertion—"our citizenship is in heaven"—provides the primary biblical text for the material in this book, it is imperative that we understand its historical background. This text has a colorful and interesting context. We will better understand the text if we understand the historical context in which it was written.

Paul wrote Philippians in the first century while he was a prisoner in Rome. He sent the letter to Christians who lived at Philippi, a city in the province of Macedonia. When Paul referred to Christians as "citizens of heaven," the believers in this city knew precisely what that meant. Why? Because Philippi was a Roman colony (Acts 16:12). The Roman Empire established colony cities in key locations across the land. These unique communities were devoted to Rome—promoting, preserving, and protecting her interests in every way as the capital city of the empire.

A Roman colony city was an outpost of Rome. No matter how far from the capital city a colony city was located, the prevailing culture was Roman through and through. The laws, the language, the customs, the views, the values, the dress, the food, the smells, and the entertainment—everything was distinctly Roman. As a resident of or a visitor to a Roman colony city, a person would feel as though he were living in Rome itself. Philippi was such a city.

When Paul wrote the words "our citizenship is in heaven" (Philippians 3:20) to Christians in Philippi, they saw the deep implications of his analogy. Those words penetrated. Loudly and clearly, they understood the message that, even though they were citizens of earth, their primary citizenship was in heaven. While they would have appreciated their temporary citizenship "here," they understood that their permanent and primary citizenship was "there"—in heaven. Even though their mailing address was in Philippi, they knew that their home city was heaven. This meant that no matter what the circumstances, conditions, or challenges of their daily lives on this earth, their character and conduct was to clearly reflect their heavenly citizenship.

The Church As a Colony of Heaven

We gain further insight into the concept of heavenly citizenship by noting the wording of James Moffatt in his paraphrase of Philippians 3:20. In a legitimate and thought-provoking way, he renders the verse with these words— "We are a colony of heaven." What are the implications of the idea that the church is to exist on earth as "a colony of heaven"? Perhaps a definition and description of "a colony" would be helpful.

Clearly, a colony is an extension or outpost of one culture in the midst of another. For Christians, heaven is our homeland—our dominant culture. Temporarily, we are residents of the distant, and sometimes hostile, setting of this earth. Yet, as "citizens of heaven" and members of "a heavenly colony," we continually seek to faithfully present and preserve the holy culture of heaven in the midst of the unholy culture of earth.

COLONY A community of people who share common roots, pursuits, meanings, and values. Even though colonists settle in a distant and sometimes hostile place, they continue to live under the control of and in the spirit of their home country. No matter how far away the residents of a colony may be planted, they continue to remember, respect, and repeat the standards and stories of their native land.

Heavenly Citizenship Requires a Birth from Above

People who are born in the United States or parented by a citizen of this country are automatically given legal status as American citizens. The process by which we become citizens of heaven has no such provisions. Bloodlines and geographical boundaries do not guarantee inclusion into the citizenry of heaven. Rather, the privilege of heavenly citizenship requires specific faith-action on the part of any and every person who seeks this high honor. There must be a direct appeal to heaven, based on the teaching of God's Word, if one is to experience and enjoy heavenly citizenship.

"Everyone who calls on the name of the Lord will be saved." How, then, can they call on the one they have not believed in? And how can they believe in the one of whom they have not heard? And how can they hear without someone preaching to them? And how can they preach unless they are sent? As it is written, "How beautiful are the feet of those who bring good news!" (Romans 10:13-15).

Entrance in the kingdom of God—heavenly citizenship—requires no less than a "new or second birth." Amazing! A person's first birth opens the way for citizenship in the universal kingdom of man, whose representative head is Adam. But, only through the new or second birth does a person enter the kingdom of God, whose head is Jesus Christ. At the time of this new birth, a marvelous transition occurs—citizenship in the old order of Adam is reduced to a secondary level, and heavenly citizenship becomes primary and pre-eminent. We actually experience immigration from the kingdom of this world to the kingdom of heaven. In fact, the transition of citizenship from earth to heaven is made official and validated when a person's name is written in the Lamb's book of life in heaven.

For he has rescued us from the dominion of darkness and brought us into the kingdom of the Son he loves, in whom we have redemption, the forgiveness of sins (Colossians 1:13, 14).

But you have come to Mount Zion, to the heavenly Jerusalem, the city of the living God. You have come to thousands upon thousands of angels in joyful assembly, to the church of the firstborn, whose names are written in heaven (Hebrews 12:22, 23).

At the time of one's new birth, a marvelous transition occurs. The person who previously was an alien and a stranger to the kingdom of God is graciously endowed with all the benefits of heavenly citizenship. He or she becomes a fellow citizen of heaven with all other obedient believers. Speaking to Christians in the first-century Ephesian church, Paul wrote

Consequently, you are no longer foreigners and aliens, but fellow citizens with God's people and members of God's household, built on the foundation of the apostles and prophets, with Christ Jesus himself as the chief cornerstone (Ephesians 2:19, 20).

What Did Jesus Teach about the Birth from Above— the New Birth?

In John 3:1-21, we learn the details surrounding an interesting encounter that Jesus had with a highly religious man who was a Pharisee and member of the Sanhedrin—the highest ranking court within the Jewish community. His name was Nicodemus. This influential man had, for some reason, taken notice of Jesus. Perhaps he had heard people telling about Jesus' miracle-working powers. He may have actually seen Jesus perform a miracle. Maybe he had heard the powerful teaching of the Master. It could be that the world of Nicodemus had been rocked by the boldness of Jesus when He entered the temple courts and "cleaned His Father's house" (John 2:12-25). Whatever the motivation, it is clear that Nicodemus was a God-seeker and desired a face-to-face encounter with the man from Nazareth—Jesus.

In a humble and complimentary way, Nicodemus approached Jesus.

He came to Jesus at night and said, "Rabbi, we know you are a teacher who has come from God. For no one could perform the miraculous signs you are doing if God were not with him" (John 3:2).

Immediately, Jesus saw through Nicodemus (John 2:24, 25) and may have shocked him with such strong and direct teaching about new birth and his need for membership in the kingdom of God. During this period, many of the Jews were under the impression that their first birth—physical birth—entitled them to special favor and fellowship with God because of their biological link to Abraham (Matthew 3:9; Luke 3:7-9; John 1:10-13). Clearly, Jesus was trying to challenge and change such ideas as He spoke these thought-provoking words to Nicodemus.

> Jesus declared, "I tell you the truth, no one can see the kingdom of God unless he is born again" (John 3:3).

The Greek word translated "born again" in our English Bibles literally means "born from above." Jesus was telling Nicodemus that heavenly citizenship can only be enjoyed when a person is ready and willing to receive new life from heaven. The strong words of Jesus confused Nicodemus.

> "How can a man be born when he is old?" Nicodemus asked. "Surely he cannot enter a second time into his mother's womb to be born!" (John 3:4).

In an effort to clarify and amplify the precise meaning of new birth, Jesus got more specific.

> Jesus answered, "I tell you the truth, no one can enter the kingdom of God unless he is born of water and the Spirit" (John 3:5).

Being "born of water and the Spirit" constitutes the means to new birth. Jesus was speaking of one birth, but He specified that there were to be two elements—water and the Spirit. To what was Jesus referring? How could a grown man like Nicodemus be born of water and the Spirit?

The words "born of water and the Spirit" refer to what would occur simultaneously in the life of Nicodemus should he, like many others, submit to the baptism being taught and practiced by John the Baptist (Matthew 3:1-17; Mark 1:1-13; Luke 3:1-22; John 1:19-28). Because he was a religious leader among the Jews, Nicodemus would have been keenly aware of the widespread teaching and evangelizing that John the Baptist was doing throughout the region of Judea. John was preaching, "a baptism of repentance for the forgiveness of sins," and crowds were coming to him to be immersed (Luke 3:3-7). Thus, Jesus was telling this man that if he, in obedient faith, would agree to have his body buried in the waters of baptism, at the same time God would immerse his inner person in the Holy Spirit. For Nicodemus, this would mean new birth.

An understanding of the historical context of that day helps us to understand this interesting conversation. Based on the Gospel accounts, it is clear that John's preaching and baptizing were the talk of the entire Jewish community at this time. His message was the hot theological topic, which explains why Jesus said what He did to this religious leader. Large numbers of Jews were flocking to John the Baptist to be baptized in the Jordan River as they anticipated the coming of the kingdom of God (Matthew 3:1-12; Mark 1:4-8).

In fact, because John was such a fascinating character and was creating such a stir in the region, the Pharisees sent a delegation to him to check out his identity and ask for his credentials to be engaging in such a widespread ministry that affected so many people (John 1:24, 25).

It is against this contextual backdrop that you should read the passage in John 3. Jesus must have known that Nicodemus was struggling with the meaning of John's message and his own personal need to prepare for the coming kingdom by being baptized in water. Jesus knew that for too long this important religious leader had, mistakenly, trusted his biological tie to Abraham. He was keenly aware that Nicodemus needed to experience a new birth. In spite of all his good qualities and strong religious leanings, Nicodemus had not yet entered the kingdom of God—a very serious problem. Thus, in a loving yet firm manner, Jesus spoke boldly to this truth-seeking man and gave him the clear command: "You must be born from above—you must be born of water and the Spirit in order to enter the kingdom of God!"

And what would be the evidence of this birth from above? How would a submissive person know that a new birth had taken place? Jesus explained to Nicodemus that the redeeming and saving work of the Holy Spirit in the new birth is similar to what happens when the wind blows objects in its path. We don't see the wind, but we do see its effects. So it is with the spiritual birth process. We don't actually see the Holy Spirit as He moves within the human heart, but we do see the life-changing results of His powerful work. Jesus explained

> Flesh gives birth to flesh, but the Spirit gives birth to spirit. You should not be surprised at my saying, "You must be born again." The wind blows wherever it pleases. You hear its sound, but you cannot tell where it comes from or where it is going. So it is with everyone born of the Spirit (John 3:6-8).

What About Us? Must We Be Born Again to Be Citizens of Heaven?

What Jesus told Nicodemus to do to be born from above is what we, too, must do in order to enjoy membership in the kingdom of God. Yes, we must be born again—born of water and the Spirit. This is confirmed in other biblical passages where sinners are told what they must do to be saved. For example, note the message of the Spirit-led apostles in Jerusalem on the Day of Pentecost. When sinners asked what they must do to be saved, Peter responded with the following words, which are strikingly similar to what Jesus said to Nicodemus in John 3:

> Peter replied, "Repent and be baptized, every one of you, in the name of Jesus Christ for the forgiveness of your sins. And you will receive the gift

of the Holy Spirit. The promise is for you and your children and for all who are far off—for all whom the Lord our God will call." With many other words he warned them; and he pleaded with them, "Save yourselves from this corrupt generation." Those who accepted his message were baptized, and about three thousand were added to their number that day (Acts 2:38-41).

Be Certain That Your Heavenly Passport Is Sealed

It is faith and trust in Jesus that leads one to genuinely repent and be immersed in water in order to receive forgiveness and the presence of the indwelling Holy Spirit. These acts of obedient faith are not—they are not—works of human merit but beautiful expressions of reliance upon the crucified and resurrected Christ.

When a sinner walks into the watery grave of baptism, he or she is saying to God and anyone else who may witness the event, "I am a sinner. I cannot save myself. I am dead in sin. I am ready to bury the old person and experience the resurrection life of Jesus. I believe in the saving work of Jesus at Calvary, and I am putting my faith in the power of His cleansing blood. I am calling upon the name of Jesus for salvation." Motivated by a spirit of faith and dependency, the sinner is buried by baptism into the benefits of Jesus' atoning death (Acts 8:35-39; 22:16; Romans 6:3-11; Galatians 3:26, 27; Colossians 2:11, 12). The blood of Jesus washes our sins away and the Holy Spirit comes to live within us (Acts 2:38, 39; 5:32; Galatians 4:6). In this beautiful faith response, one is being born of water and the Spirit—born again—born from above.

Even in the case of Jesus Himself, there was a direct connection in time between His baptism and the coming of the Holy Spirit (Matthew 3:13-17; Mark 1:9, 11; Luke 3:21, 22). Other passages that help us to understand the significance of being born of water and the Spirit include Titus 3:5-7; Matthew 28:18-20; and Mark 16:15, 16.

Be a citizen of heaven. Make sure that your heavenly passport is clearly sealed with the cleansing blood of the Lamb of God. This is very important as you make your appeal for heavenly citizenship and enjoy the blessings and benefits thereof.

Heavenly Citizenship—a Present Reality

Do we see that when Paul wrote those words, "Our citizenship is in heaven," he was not speaking about a future promise, but a present reality? The content of this study is not as much about going to heaven some day as it is about living as citizens of heaven today. Because we hold the high and holy citizenship of heaven, we are called by God to live high and holy lives on earth.

But you are a chosen people, a royal priesthood, a holy nation, a people belonging to God, that you may declare the praises of him who called you out of darkness into his wonderful light. Once you were not a people, but now you are the people of God; once you had not received mercy, but now you have received mercy. Dear friends, I urge you, as aliens and strangers in the world, to abstain from sinful desires, which war against your soul. Live such good lives among the pagans that, though they accuse you of doing wrong, they may see your good deeds and glorify God on the day he visits us (1 Peter 2:9-12).

FOR FURTHER DISCUSSION AND INTERACTION

1   Discuss the depth of your understanding of "heavenly citizenship." Has the principle been adequately taught in our churches? How firmly has the biblical principle gripped you as a Christian? To what extent has this concept influenced your daily views, values, convictions, and behaviors?

2   How meaningful to you is the song, "This World Is Not My Home"? Explain your response.

3   Do you agree with the assertion that we are to be Christians first and Americans second? When is patriotism healthy? When could loyalty to the state become unhealthy?

4   Identify five practical ways that a Christian's daily character and conduct can reflect his or her heavenly citizenship and culture.

5   Paul used the benefits of his Roman citizenship to spread the gospel in the first-century world (Acts 16:37-40; 22:22-29). Are there ways for us to use our legal rights as American citizens to promote the proclamation of the gospel? As an American, do you see signs that changing legal policies may hinder or even block our constitutional rights to openly proclaim and practice the Christian faith in the present or future?

6   Moffatt's rendering of Philippians 3:20 refers to the church as "a colony of heaven." What do those words mean to you? Would this view of God's church change the way modern-day Christians see themselves and their mission in the world? If yes, explain why?

7   Our first birth entitles us to earthly citizenship. Our second birth, of water and the Spirit, opens the way for us to enjoy heavenly citizenship. Discuss the significance of your second birth as a transition point when your heavenly citizenship became primary and your earthly citizenship became secondary. Even in our day, is it still essential for a person to be "born of water and the Spirit" in order to be a citizen of heaven?

8   Our modern-day religious setting is one in which carefully reasoned out biblical doctrine is frequently devalued and freedom to believe as one chooses is valued. In view of this reality, how do you think Jesus would be viewed in our day if He were to approach a highly religious person and boldly say, "I tell you the truth, no one can enter the kingdom of God unless he is born of water and the Spirit . . . You must be born again" (John 3:5-7)?

9 Have we tended to view heavenly citizenship as a future promise rather than a present reality? How has the material in Chapter 1 reinforced or changed your view in this regard?

CHAPTER 2

The Nature and Challenge of Earthly Residency

We Are Strangers and Aliens in This World

The clear message of Scripture is that Christians are strangers and resident-aliens in this world. Throughout the centuries, men and women of God have understood and freely declared that this world is not their home.

> All these people were still living by faith when they died. They did not receive the things promised; they only saw them and welcomed them from a distance. And they admitted that they were aliens and strangers on earth. People who say such things show that they are looking for a country of their own. If they had been thinking of the country they had left, they would have had opportunity to return. Instead, they were longing for a better country—a heavenly one. Therefore God is not ashamed to be called their God, for he has prepared a city for them (Hebrews 11:13-16).

> To God's elect, strangers in the world (1 Peter 1:1).

> Since you call on a Father who judges each man's work impartially, live your lives as strangers here in reverent fear (1 Peter 1:17).

> I urge you, as aliens and strangers in the world, to abstain from sinful desires, which war against your soul (1 Peter 2:11).

A stranger is someone who is out of his or her natural environment and belongs to a different people with a different culture—frequently speaking a different language or having a distinct accent. Often, a stranger is recognized as one who practices different values and ethical standards. As citizens of heaven, we are "strangers" in this world.

Similarly, an alien is a foreign-born individual whose beliefs and behaviors are likely to be very different from the natives with whom he or she shares space. Aliens are sometimes viewed with caution or suspicion because they are different from the norm. Many foreigners would tell us that they have not been freely accepted or trusted by people of the home country. In view of these realities, we should feel especially sad when we think of the deep pain Jesus must have felt. "He came to that which was his own, but his own did not receive him" (John 1:11). Believers in Jesus are referred to as "aliens" in this present world.

With our citizenship in heaven and our ties to this world changed, we should have an entirely different perspective on how we spend the few remaining years that we will have as residents of this earth. It is important for us to know how to conduct ourselves in an alien culture. The guidelines in this chapter will offer helpful insights and practical information on immigration survival for members of Jesus' church—a colony of heaven.

1 WE MUST ACCEPT OUR ALIEN STATUS IN THIS WORLD.

As citizens of heaven, we must own our new identity on earth as resident-aliens. Even though this description of Christians fits with the message of Scripture, it can stretch or even rip through the comfort zones of some very religious people. The view that Christians are strangers in this world is far too radical and thus unacceptable to some professing believers. For years, churchgoers have blended comfortably into the dominant culture of the world around them. Little, if anything, was different between believers and unbelievers. Thus, to some, the idea of Christians living as foreigners on this planet is a thought entirely foreign to their way of thinking. Have we been living, for too long in a time of shallow commitment and easy discipleship? The words of Jesus must silence and overrule the critics.

> But he continued, "You [non-believers] are from below; I am from above. You are of this world; I am not of this world" (John 8:23).

> If you [followers of Jesus] belonged to the world, it would love you as its own. As it is, you do not belong to the world, but I have chosen you out of the world. That is why the world hates you (John 15:19).

> I have given them [followers of Jesus] your word and the world has hated them, for they are not of the world any more than I am of the world (John 17:14).

> They [followers of Jesus] are not of the world, even as I am not of it (John 17:16).

A reluctance to accept our alien status as Christians may signal a need for us to reexamine the basic meaning of conversion to Jesus Christ. When our Lord called for sinners to follow Him, His practice was to stop them in their tracks and ask, "Have you counted the cost? Do you understand the deep life-commitment you are making?" He knew that a transferal of one's citizenship from earth to heaven was no insignificant step. He wanted them to be fully informed.

> Large crowds were traveling with Jesus, and turning to them He said: "If anyone comes to me and does not hate his father and mother, his wife and children, his brothers and sisters—yes, even his own life—he cannot be my disciple. And anyone who does not carry his cross and follow me cannot be my disciple. Suppose one of you wants to build a tower. Will he not first sit down and estimate the cost to see if he has enough money to complete it? For if he lays the foundation and is not able to finish it, everyone who sees it will ridicule him, saying, 'This fellow began to build and was not able to finish.' Or suppose a king is about to go to war against another king. Will he not first sit down and consider whether he is able with ten thousand men to oppose the one coming against him with twenty thousand? If he is not able, he will send a delegation while the other is still a long way off and will ask for terms of peace. In the same way, any of you who does not give up everything he has cannot be my disciple" (Luke 14:25-33).

There can be no denial that discipleship in the kingdom of God calls for a radical change of life and emphasis. When we submit to the lordship of Jesus, we are enrolling as citizens of heaven—our names are written there (Luke 10:20; Hebrews 12:23; Philippians 3:20). We are becoming part of an unseen order—the innumerable company of the saints in heaven that surrounds us even now—a company that is seen only with eyes of faith (Hebrews 12:1, 2, 22, 23). As obedient followers of Christ, we are striving to learn a lifestyle that is free of fleshly addictions and enslavement to our physical senses (Philippians 3:18-20; Colossians 3:1-10). We are experiencing the sweet taste of heaven and we long for more (Hebrews 6:4, 5; Philippians 1:21, 22). We are learning to live daily with an eager expectation and anticipation of our coming Lord and the eternal inheritance He has reserved for us (Philippians 3:20, 21; 1 Peter 1:4-9; Hebrews 10:32-34). There is no question. This is a huge step and one that we must personally own.

2 WE MUST UNDERSTAND THAT AS ALIENS WE ARE DIFFERENT FROM THE WORLD.

How long has it been since you encountered a person from a culture different from your own? What did you notice? In most cases, it does not take long to recognize the fact that he or she thinks and acts differently than you do.

As strangers and aliens in this world, we are to think and act differently than the natives of this world. Never again will we fit in quite like we once did. So much has changed. We speak a new language, and the old vernacular of this world is now foreign to us. Through the Word of God, we now have new understandings, and the old understandings no longer make sense. What once seemed so desirable is now seen as destructive. Even our definition of success has changed. What was once so valuable to us may now be seen as worthless. Believers in Jesus Christ, rather than belonging to the dark world around them, are "a people belonging to God...[who have been called] out of darkness into his wonderful light" (1 Peter 2:9).

> Dear friends, I urge you, as aliens and strangers in the world, to abstain from sinful desires, which war against your soul. Live such good lives among the pagans that, though they accuse you of doing wrong, they may see your good deeds and glorify God on the day he visits us (1 Peter 2:11, 12).

> Therefore, I urge you, brothers, in view of God's mercy, to offer your bodies as living sacrifices, holy and pleasing to God—this is your spiritual act of worship. Do not conform any longer to the pattern of this world, but be transformed by the renewing of your mind. Then you will be able to test and approve what God's will is—his good, pleasing and perfect will (Romans 12:1, 2).

Again, how did Jesus pray for His followers just before He left them to return to the Father?

> My prayer is not that you take them out of the world but that you protect them from the evil one. They are not of the world, even as I am not of it (John 17:15, 16).

Heavenly citizenship is a call to holiness. The word "holy" means to be set apart. If you are apart from the world, you cannot be a part of it as you once were. Holy people can never fit into an environment of unholiness. This explains why members of the colony of heaven are likely, at times, to experience feelings of loneliness and alienation—even rejection. As someone has said of Christians living in a godless society, "Our days of being cool are over." In a dark world, we are called to be lights for God (Philippians 2:14-16; 1 John 2:15-17).

> For you were once darkness, but now you are light in the Lord. Live as children of light (for the fruit of the light consists in all goodness, righteousness and truth) and find out what pleases the Lord. Have nothing to do with the fruitless deeds of darkness, but rather expose them. For it is shameful even

to mention what the disobedient do in secret. But everything exposed by the light becomes visible, for it is light that makes everything visible. This is why it is said: "Wake up, O sleeper, rise from the dead, and Christ will shine on you." Be very careful, then, how you live—not as unwise but as wise, making the most of every opportunity, because the days are evil (Ephesians 5:8-16).

Being separated from the world will irritate and infuriate some. Jesus predicted this.

If the world hates you, keep in mind that it hated me first. If you belonged to the world, it would love you as its own. As it is, you do not belong to the world, but I have chosen you out of the world. That is why the world hates you (John 15:18, 19).

Someone might counter these ideas with the important and valid observation that, as believers, we are to identify with outsiders in an effort to more effectively bring the light of the gospel to them. Paul, the Jew, was constantly crossing cultural boundaries to gain the ear of his listeners. Yet in crossing over, he did not give in when it came to matters of eternal truth and morality.

Though I am free and belong to no man, I make myself a slave to everyone, to win as many as possible. To the Jews I became like a Jew, to win the Jews. To those under the law I became like one under the law (though I myself am not under the law), so as to win those under the law. To those not having the law I became like one not having the law (though I am not free from God's law but am under Christ's law), so as to win those not having the law. To the weak I became weak, to win the weak. I have become all things to all men so that by all possible means I might save some. I do all this for the sake of the gospel that I may share in its blessings (1 Corinthians 9:19-23.)

Becoming all things to all men does not require us to obscure the fact that we are citizens of heaven. In our legitimate efforts to bend over and communicate with the world, we must not lose our balance and fall in. We can never practice lying in order to reach liars. Compromising our principles in order to reach those who live in rebellion to God is never acceptable. While it is desirable to be relevant in our efforts to gain the ear of the secular world, it is never permissible to change the gospel message in an effort to make it palatable to the secular mind. The saying, "When in Rome, do as the Romans do," does not apply when Roman belief or behavior is contrary to the life and spirit of Jesus. Our conduct must always match our citizenship (1 John 4:17).

Our attempts to be relevant must never obscure or obstruct the clarity of supreme loyalty to Jesus Christ. Spiritual truths are likely to be considered as foolishness to those who have unspiritual minds (1 Corinthians 1:18-31; 2:14). We could never expect that a mind controlled by the sinful nature would cheerfully embrace the principles and practices embodied in the Beatitudes (Matthew 5:1-12; Romans 8:5-8). How could the Lord's Supper ever be relevant or meaningful to a godless citizen of this world?

Citizens of heaven cannot blend with this secular world without losing their heavenly citizenship. This is made clear again and again in the Scriptures. During our earthly pilgrimage, we must continually battle the temptation to abandon our status as strangers in this world only to settle down and integrate into the host society. As residents on this earth, we can never live as permanent homesteaders and have friendly connections with the evil ways of this world.

> You adulterous people, don't you know that friendship with the world is hatred toward God? Anyone who chooses to be a friend of the world becomes an enemy of God (James 4:4).

3 AS ALIENS, WE LIVE ON EARTH WITH A LINGERING SENSE OF INCOMPLETENESS AND A LONGING FOR THE HOMELAND OF HEAVEN.

After affirming our heavenly citizenship in Philippians 3:20, it is not coincidental that Paul adds these words:

> And we eagerly await a Savior from there, the Lord Jesus Christ.

Humans work so hard to achieve happiness and discover fulfillment in this world. Yet, in spite of our best efforts, we never seem to find the deep-down, lasting satisfaction that we crave. But, we don't give up easily. We are determined. So, we build bigger houses. We buy finer cars. We go for makeovers and wear fancier clothes and more expensive jewelry. Happiness is out there somewhere—we just have to find it.

We apply those secret formulas in miracle-working cosmetics that promise to make us look like we just drank from the fountain of youth. We further expand and diversify our portfolios and then ride the roller coaster of mood swings as the stock market ebbs and flows. With excitement and anticipation, we travel to exotic places, but frequently return home feeling weary with less money and more frustrations. These and a 1,001 other plans and projects we pursue in a mad search for inner peace. Yet we continue to feel that gnawing sense of emptiness and incompleteness. And we wonder to ourselves, "Is this all there is?"

Yet there really is something better. There is reason to be optimistic and hopeful! Imagine a scene where the census taker is at your door asking the question, "In what country do you hold primary citizenship?" With great joy and anticipation, the believer in Jesus can confidently and joyfully reply, "Yes! I am a citizen of heaven and I am eagerly awaiting a Savior from there who will transform my lowly body so that it will be like His glorious body!"

This changes the way we view and cope with the troubles and trials of this earth. What once depressed and defeated us now gives us greater determination to press on!

> Therefore we do not lose heart. Though outwardly we are wasting away, yet inwardly we are being renewed day by day. For our light and momentary troubles are achieving for us an eternal glory that far outweighs them all. So we fix our eyes not on what is seen, but on what is unseen. For what is seen is temporary, but what is unseen is eternal (2 Corinthians 4:16-18).

The Bible teaches that we live in tents—our bodies (2 Corinthians 5:1-5). No wonder we are so uncomfortable. Tents leak. Tents tear. Tents smell. Tents blow away. Tents are uncomfortable and inadequate for protection from the elements. Tents can never protect us from danger. So, in tents, "[W]e groan and are burdened...[We long] to be clothed with our heavenly dwelling" (v. 4), which will be the new bodies, suitable for eternity, which God will provide for us at the time of the final resurrection (1 Corinthians 15:35-58). Until that time comes, prepare to do some groaning, yet live in joyful and hopeful anticipation of the final day of redemption.

> I consider that our present sufferings are not worth comparing with the glory that will be revealed in us. The creation waits in eager expectation for the sons of God to be revealed. For the creation was subjected to frustration, not by its own choice, but by the will of the one who subjected it, in hope that the creation itself will be liberated from its bondage to decay and brought into the glorious freedom of the children of God. We know that the whole creation has been groaning as in the pains of childbirth right up to the present time. Not only so, but we ourselves, who have the firstfruits of the Spirit, groan inwardly as we wait eagerly for our adoption as sons, the redemption of our bodies. For in this hope we were saved. But hope that is seen is no hope at all. Who hopes for what he already has? But if we hope for what we do not yet have, we wait for it patiently (Romans 8:18-25).

FOR FURTHER DISCUSSION AND INTERACTION

1 Is the concept of Christians being foreigners or aliens in this world a foreign thought to you? To what extent has this idea been a part of your previous thinking and practice?

2 What feelings or emotions begin to surface within you when you ponder the implications of being an alien in this world for Christ—fear, readiness, confusion, motivation, grief, anger, anticipation, or others?

3 Is it difficult or easy for us to live in the world while remaining separate from the world? If you maintain that it is difficult, give reasons for the difficulty of this challenge.

4 Do you agree or disagree with the idea that we may have been living in a time of shallow commitment and easy discipleship? Have too many Christians blended into the dominant culture of the world in an unhealthy and sinful way?

5 Discuss the meaning of holiness—being set apart from the world. At the same time, explore ideas related to the challenge of approaching our culture with relevancy and methods that are effective. Where are the lines to be drawn in the tension that exists between what is revealed (biblical truths) and what is relevant (methods that seem to work)? What makes this such a difficult and sensitive area for Christian believers?

6 How bold should children of the light be in confronting and exposing the works of darkness? What are the implications of such actions in today's society? How can this concept affect our families and our standing in the daily workplace? Can you point to a person who has dared to question and challenge the views and values of this secular world? What were the consequences of such decisions?

7 What practical and workable steps could we and should we take in today's church to encourage more believers to be bold and courageous in walking the narrow way that leads to life even while living in the midst of a hostile culture?

8 You have heard the phrase, "homesick for heaven." Share what this phrase means to you. How deep is your longing for the homeland of heaven? How eagerly do you await the Lord's return? It would be good to have an aging saint share his or her personal view of and longing for the homeland of heaven. (Be sure to have plenty of tissues on hand.)

9 In death, we move out of our tents—our physical bodies. At the time of the final resurrection, we move into an eternal house in heaven not built by human hands (2 Corinthians 5:1-5). What does this transition mean to you? Discuss this truth in terms of your Christian hope.

CHAPTER 3

Heavenly Citizenship in a Culture That Is Becoming More Adversarial

Citizens of Heaven in Modern-Day America

Unquestionably, many of the founders of the United States of America were people with Christian convictions, confidence in the Bible as the Word of God, and faith in the power and value of prayer. They left their motherland, not to create a nation that was separated from God, but to separate themselves from a religious system that was persecuting them because of their faith in God.

For those old enough to recall, there was a time when many viewed the United States as a Christian nation. The predominant culture was heavily influenced by Judeo-Christian teachings. God's fingerprints were all over our founding documents and governing principles. The confident assumption on the part of many Christians—however misinformed they may have been—was that the culture was ours. Those who tried to counter this culture were viewed as radicals and not taken seriously. Some operated on the assumption that to grow up American was to grow up Christian. Many of the conditions that existed across the land seemed to validate this assumption. A biblical emphasis was so strong that Christians, for the most part, simply did not feel like foreigners in a strange land.

My own personal experience of growing up in the southern Bible belt may serve to illustrate the point. Hopefully, this picture of one man's experience will give the reader, regardless of age, a cultural snapshot of a country that, for many years, encouraged Christian principles and practices.

A Specific Example of a Jesus-Friendly Neighborhood

Yes, there was a time when it seemed that America would always be a Christian nation. Political policies and cultural practices seemed to validate this widely-held view. For example, when I was growing up in a suburb of Nashville, Tennessee, it was easy to think that the church, the home, the state, and the school formed a consortium that worked together to instill and uphold Christian principles as a way of life.

In my boyhood home, both parents were Christians. In those days, divorces rarely occurred. In the local neighborhood setting, there was little or no concern about thieves or thugs who might try to steal or inflict bodily harm. Electronic security systems did not exist—who needed them? In my childhood dwelling, there was no key to lock the back door. We lived in a safe and secure environment. In fact, as young children, we were encouraged by our parents to meet and greet strangers in public places. Neighbors knew neighbors by name. Rarely did any move away. On hot summer nights, friends would gather in yards and on front porches. With no air conditioning, the outside air made the heat more bearable. During these neighborhood gatherings, relationships were formed. The adults talked and the children played.

In the vast majority of these homes, dads went to work daily to provide the family's livelihood, and moms stayed at home to care for the children. On a typical Sunday morning, cars were coming and going as the majority of families attended Bible classes and a worship assembly of a local church. For the most part, it was a neighborhood of shared moral values and standards. Kids were taught respect for authority and accountability to God.

At the local elementary school, we read the Bible each morning and prayed aloud—moments of silence were unheard of. We called it prayer. Patriotic songs were sung and the Pledge of Allegiance to the flag was repeated. Even though this was a public school under the supervision of the U.S. Department of Education, prayer and Bible reading were never in question. School administrators intentionally avoided scheduling public meetings on Wednesday nights so that students and faculty could participate in prayer meetings and Bible studies in their local churches. In fact, the principal and the vast majority of the teachers openly lived by Christian standards themselves. Never do I recall hearing or reading of a mass shooting at a school or anywhere else.

In the marketplaces of my boyhood environment, there were no pornographic magazines or videos on store shelves. In the one community theater, the movies were rated G and suitable for the entire family to watch—no steamy bedroom scenes or bloody violence. Now and then, a cowboy might caress and kiss his horse, but nothing more than this. Even Hollywood seemed to be in touch with the acceptable standards of the culture. Alcohol was available, but only in the few liquor stores scattered across the city. On Sunday, all gas stations, grocery stores, and other retail outlets were closed so that employees could go to church and families could be together. Public meetings and sporting events were frequently preceded by prayer in the name of Jesus. This was the norm, and no one objected.

More detail could be added, but this brief cultural snapshot will suffice for giving the reader a glimpse of what life was like for at least one individual living in the American culture just a few years ago. Granted, the conditions would vary for another person living at the same time in another place. However, this account does provide the picture and pattern of an environment that was generally tolerant and supportive of Judeo-Christian views and values for its citizens. In such a setting, it is easy to see why many people assumed that America was and would always be a Christian nation. Yet the undeniable reality is that what was, no longer is.

America Today and the Christian Faith

Obviously, many cultural conditions have drastically changed. Today, many believe that any mention of the God of the Bible should be limited or even barred from the public arena. Growing numbers of people who sit in positions of leadership and influence view the Bible with fear and suspicion. More and more, the voice of God and the truth of His Word are being silenced in this land. To teach the Scriptures as the inspired Word of God and the authoritative standard for determining right and wrong is viewed by many as an act of gross ignorance. Evolutionary teaching is widely accepted as fact. While the Bible declares that God created man and that humans are ultimately accountable to Him, the secular world looks upon man as an animal that evolved over millions of years and is accountable only to himself.

Today's culture is promoting a worldview that encourages anti-family values, teaches moral relativism, and encourages sexual conduct that is primarily concerned about using safe contraception methods in an environment of open mating. The Bible refers to adultery as a sin (Hebrews 13:4). Secular humanists mildly call it an extramarital affair. The view that marriage is the union of one man and one woman is viewed as homophobic and full of hatred and intolerance. What God refers to as a moral perversion (homosexuality), the modern culture calls an alternative lifestyle (Romans 1:24-27). The lives of innocent babies are sacrificed, while freedom of choice is shielded. In fact, it is not uncommon to hear political activists demanding that we save the trees, while, at the same time, they call for the right to kill babies. Sadly, we are living in a day when the biblical views that sin is real and that sinners must turn to Jesus Christ for salvation are ridiculed and stigmatized as archaic superstitions.

Obviously, the cultural environment of today has become much more hostile to the Christian culture of heaven. At the core of these issues is the central problem mentioned by Paul as he described the moral and spiritual sickness that plagued the people of his day:

"There is no fear of God before their eyes" (Romans 3:18).

No wonder Christians cannot feel at home in this world. While the culture of this land was never really ours as some may have assumed, we need only to listen to our daily (bad) news broadcasts to be reminded of the serious problems facing today's, so-called, liberated culture. We have become so free in this society that many are feeling the need to put bars over their doors and windows.

As members of the colony of heaven, we can no longer be so foolish as to think that we can depend on the state, the school, or the culture-at-large to help mold the values and views of the people with whom we live. The sad reality is that we cannot even count on some in the religious community of our day who are tolerating and teaching anti-Christian ideas. Citizens of heaven must return to their biblical roots and boldly counter the culture of this world by teaching a different view of authority, a different definition of morality, and even a different set of daily value judgments. In the name of Jesus Christ, we must stand up boldly and speak up courageously.

> For you were once darkness, but now you are light in the Lord. Live as children of light (for the fruit of the light consists in all goodness, righteousness and truth) and find out what pleases the Lord. Have nothing to do with the fruitless deeds of darkness, but rather expose them (Ephesians 5:8-11).

Seeing This World through the Eyes of Christ

Jesus, too, lived in a culture that was spiritually and morally bankrupt. With sensitivity and emotion, He responded to the unbelieving people of His day. Can you sense the sorrow in His voice as He spoke while looking over the rebellious city of Jerusalem, "If you, even you, had only known on this day what would bring you peace—but now it is hidden from your eyes" (Luke 19:41, 42)? With eyes wet with tears, He cried, "O, Jerusalem, Jerusalem, you who kill the prophets and stone those sent to you, how often I have longed to gather your children together, as a hen gathers her chicks under her wings, but you were not willing" (Matthew 23:37). With great compassion, He saw the masses as "sheep without a shepherd" (Matthew 9: 35, 36). Are we seeing the people of our cities and towns with the eyes of Jesus? Do we love the people of our day with the love of the Lord (Philippians 1:8)? Is anyone weeping and mourning for those who are trapped in this world because their spiritual passports will not allow passage beyond the border of this earth into the full benefits of heavenly citizenship?

As Paul wrote so joyfully and hopefully to the Philippian believers regarding their heavenly citizenship, He also expressed His deep sorrow for those who were not citizens of heaven.

For, as I have often told you before and now say again even with tears, many live as enemies of the cross of Christ. Their destiny is destruction, their god is their stomach, and their glory is in their shame. Their mind is on earthly things. But our citizenship is in heaven. And we eagerly await a Savior from there, the Lord Jesus Christ (Philippians 3:18-20).

The Corrupting Power in Today's Culture

Clearly, there are destructive and unhealthy forces at work in this world in which we live as residents. These powerful forces are the work of the enemy, Satan, and his demonic agents (Ephesians 6:10-12). Having done battle with this enemy during His lifetime, Jesus prayed for His disciples before He left them, "My prayer is not that you take them out of the world but that you protect them from the evil one" (John 17:15). We know something of the enemy's tactics, because we were once under his control.

> As for you, you were dead in your transgressions and sins, in which you used to live when you followed the ways of this world and of the ruler of the kingdom of the air, the spirit who is now at work in those who are disobedient. All of us also lived among them at one time, gratifying the cravings of our sinful nature and following its desires and thoughts. Like the rest, we were by nature objects of wrath (Ephesians 2:1-3).

> At one time we too were foolish, disobedient, deceived and enslaved by all kinds of passions and pleasures. We lived in malice and envy, being hated and hating one another (Titus 3:3).

This enemy is still on the scene—wounded and facing ultimate defeat (Colossians 2:15)—yet he continues to be dangerous and determined.

> Be self-controlled and alert. Your enemy the devil prowls around like a roaring lion looking for someone to devour (1 Peter 5:8).

We know that we are children of God, and that the whole world is under the control of the evil one (1 John 5:19).

A Reminder Regarding Our Present Mission— Avoiding Two Extremes

So, what is our mission in and to the country of our first birth? While it is not possible to fix the sinful world and create a "Christian utopia" on this earth, still there is much for us to do during our residency here. Two extremes are to be avoided. One extreme would be to live in total oblivion to our heavenly connection and citizenship—to be completely immersed in the earthly culture and to bear no Christian distinctiveness. The other extreme would be to live in total detachment and isolation from the affairs of this earth—treating the world as an area that is off-limits for Christians. Paul clarified such matters for the first-century Corinthian church as he explained the process of withdrawing fellowship from a rebellious and sinful brother or sister in the Lord.

> I have written you in my letter not to associate with sexually immoral people—not at all meaning the people of this world who are immoral, or the greedy and swindlers, or idolaters. In that case you would have to leave this world. But now I am writing you that you must not associate with anyone who calls himself a brother but is sexually immoral or greedy, an idolater or a slanderer, a drunkard or a swindler. With such a man do not even eat (1 Corinthians 5:9-11).

We are to live in the world, yet not be of the world, while we fulfill our mission to the world by living as a savoring influence in the culture that surrounds us.

> "You are the salt of the earth. But if the salt loses its saltiness, how can it be made salty again? It is no longer good for anything, except to be thrown out and trampled by men. You are the light of the world. A city on a hill cannot be hidden. Neither do people light a lamp and put it under a bowl. Instead they put it on its stand, and it gives light to everyone in the house. In the same way, let your light shine before men, that they may see your good deeds and praise your Father in heaven" (Matthew 5:13-16).

A few years back, visitors to our national parks were encouraged to leave them cleaner than they found them. Our challenge is to bring the culture of heaven to this earth and leave it better than we found it through the influence of Jesus Christ. This can only happen when our earthly conduct matches our heavenly citizenship.

FOR FURTHER DISCUSSION AND INTERACTION

1   Over the years, many have boldly declared that America is a Christian nation. From your vantage point, do you tend to agree or disagree? Has your viewpoint on this matter changed from what it was? Why?

2   Refer back to the account of the author's boyhood days in Nashville, Tennessee. Identify five factors in that environment that would tend to have a positive impact and promote a Christian lifestyle. Compare your responses with conditions of the present day.

3   Discuss the importance and necessity of having a healthy fear of God. What does it mean to fear God and how would this trait make a difference in today's world? Do you feel that the fear of God is being properly taught and adequately modeled by today's Christian community?

4   "Freedom" is an important word and valuable principle in our country. Many precious lives have been given to provide and protect our freedom. What does freedom mean to you as a citizen of this land? How could the concept of freedom be misused and actually lead to bondage?

5   To what extent do we grieve over the sinful conditions in the world around us? Is this an area where growth and greater sensitivity is needed? How can we improve in this matter? What do you feel as you look out on a culture that does not know the love and peace of God?

6   Is Satan a daily reality to you? Are you conscious on a daily basis of spiritual warfare? How can we deepen our awareness of Satan's presence and more effectively do battle with him? What tactics are especially effective in your life for combating the enemy?

7   Satan has tactics and schemes, and he uses them to cause damage and destruction. Identify one tactic of the enemy that you see him using in a powerful way in today's society.

8   Someone has said, "This world is a bridge. A wise person will pass over it, but not build his house on it." How does this saying match with some of the ideas covered in this chapter?

9   Using the analogy of an embassy in a foreign country, explain how the church is to function in this world. Share your insights on the meaning of Christians living as "ambassadors of Christ" in this world (2 Corinthians 5:20).

CITIZENS OF HEAVEN—RESIDENTS OF EARTH

CHAPTER 4

Human Philosophies That Shape the Culture of This World

Attempting to Understand the Culture We Serve

The first step in preparing for life in a new culture is to educate yourself about the country to which you are moving. What is going on in today's culture where Christians live as alien residents? It is easy enough to see that something powerful is messing with the minds and values of people, but do we know what it is? Correctly, we say that "Satan and sin are at work," but are we able to put a specific label on some of the more prevalent social philosophies that, like rip currents hidden beneath the surface, are sucking people under and taking them down to physical, emotional, and spiritual destruction? Something is seriously wrong, but what is it?

Look around. Many people are empty, lonely, and broken. Frustration, anger, and hatred grip the lives of our daily associates. Folks are turning to—you name it—for relief, but the pain does not go away. They long to find the clear and peaceful waters of life, but feel trapped in the murky waters of hopelessness or the rough and dangerous seas of failure. Yes, Satan the destroyer is at work; but can we specifically identify some of the deceitful tricks and tactics he is using as powerful undercurrents to pull his victims down and under? He offers people freedom and pleasure, but frequently leads them into bondage and misery. How does he do it? Can we pinpoint some of the dangerous philosophies with which the enemy is baiting and hooking the people of our day?

If we are to speak convincingly as we attempt to offer a lifeline of hope to people around us, it is important for us to see through the appealing lies that many are embracing as they "go with the flow" of a failing culture. It is important that we, for offensive and defensive purposes, take time to understand some of the popular views that have shaped and are continuing to shape the beliefs and behaviors of the people we are here to serve.

So I tell you this, and insist on it in the Lord, that you must no longer live as the Gentiles do, in the futility of their thinking. They are darkened in their understanding and separated from the life of God because of the ignorance that is in them due to the hardening of their hearts. Having lost all sensitivity, they have given themselves over to sensuality so as to indulge in every kind of impurity, with a continual lust for more (Ephesians 4:17-19).

Recognize the Destructive Power of SECULARISM

Daily, we are walking through a culture that has been highly secularized. Are we aware? Do we know what this means? Do we see these forces at work and grasp their seriousness? The mindset of secularism is having a major impact on the way people are believing and behaving—both leaders and followers in today's society. We must expose this philosophy so clearly that its presence is detected and its power is recognized. What a shame for such an evil philosophy to have a chokehold on us, and we don't even know it.

The word "secular" comes from a Latin word, which means world or this present age. Even this simple definition provides a glimpse into the nature of secularism. It is a philosophy that attempts to place all emphasis on this world and rules out the existence of supernatural reality—God. Belief in God is thought to be the highest form of self-deception. Supernatural reality is nothing more than the result of human imagination. Secularists insist that, "Reality is what you can perceive with the five senses." Because we cannot see, hear, taste, feel, or smell God; and because His existence cannot be verified and validated through the scientific process, we cannot accept His reality. Human reasoning and logic are the only valid tools for understanding and comprehending what is true and real. Think about it. Are we not seeing this philosophy lived out every day? But are we really "seeing" it?

As secularism gradually works its way into and through a culture over a long period of time, God and His influence are dismissed and ultimately eliminated. Religious faith is viewed as something that can only be private and personal—any public appeal to behavior based on allegiance to God is viewed as un-American. Secularists are set free from a cumbersome belief in a Creator God to whom they are accountable and responsible. There is no life after this one—no heaven and no hell. Add it all up. God, Bible, heaven, hell—they are all fiction.

The secularists' code of right and wrong dictates that humans conduct themselves ethically when dealing with each other so that harm is non existent or minimal. However, they reject any objective code such as the Bible that can be used to influence peoples' behavior. Ultimately, each human being is responsible for his or her own actions and would never submit to the dictates of a God who is unknown and unknowable in a scientific way. Are we really willing to trust each human, without the wisdom and guidance of God, to decide and act responsibly? Talk about blind faith! How is this approach working for us in today's society?

Christians must understand that secularism has had a dominant role in the western culture for a long period of time. It is the umbrella philosophy of our day under which many other godless philosophies survive and thrive. Its influence is so pervasive that it reaches into every area of our society. You can see its presence in the courts, the government, the media, our educational system, the entertainment world, the workplace, and the home. And we should ask, "Is the influence of secularism affecting our lives as members of the colony of heaven?"

Secularism is man's attempt to move God out of His place of superiority and authority, which should make us aware of the need to

Recognize the Destructive Power of HUMANISM

As secularism moves God out of His place of superiority and authority, guess who moves into that space? Yes, humans!

As the Creator is pushed aside, the creature tends to take center stage! This brings into focus another dominant philosophy that shapes today's society—humanism. Look closely at this word—"hu-MAN-ism." When you see what lies at its center, it then becomes a picture-word that is self-explanatory. Always, secularism is the forerunner of humanism—the two philosophies go together as a natural sequence. In fact, a good way to refer to the evil process being described in this chapter is "Secularistic Humanism."

Humanists believe that people should look to themselves—not God—for answers to the questions of life. By reasoning outward from themselves, they believe that humans, alone, can decide how best to judge all matters. Obviously, this puts humans in the position of being self-ruled—not God-ruled.

Humanists believe that the world evolved out of chaos—and the world is itself chaos until, through man's own genius and reasoning ability, he finds ways to control and organize it. There is no divine purpose or providence. We must save ourselves from ourselves and do it for ourselves. There are no absolute standards for good and evil—all acts are morally neutral except for their influence on others. In fact, humans must create their own standards for right and wrong, and be comfortable changing the rules as the needs of culture dictate. How strange! Someone said, "Once we believed in God, then we didn't believe in God, and now we think we are God!"

As God is moved out and as humans assume the place of superiority and authority, other human behaviors begin to appear. This points to the need for us to

Recognize the Destructive Power of RELATIVISM

This popular way of thinking denies that there is any absolute truth that is universally binding on everyone. Since everything is temporal and subject to continual change, nothing absolute exists. Everything is relative.

Picture a massive ball of culture that rolls through the centuries. Some big chunks fall off over a period of time and other large pieces are added to the ball as it continually rolls. Every part of this cultural ball is subject to change and modification—no portion is absolute, fixed, and permanent. And, as far as personal decisions regarding which part of this cultural ball will have meaning and significance in a person's life, the advocate of relativism would argue that this is entirely up to each individual. Truth for one person will not necessarily be truth for another person. Truth is determined by each person's interpretation and subjective experience.

The bottom line is that according to the philosophy of relativism, each individual must examine the facts as he or she sees them. Then each person decides for himself or herself what is true and what is false. Everything is relative. Each person is "a law unto himself or herself." What is true and right for me will not necessarily be true and right for you. What is true and right for me today will not necessarily be true and right for me tomorrow. Relativism is a system of faith in humans rather than faith in God. In a serious way, this way of thinking undermines and threatens the foundational principle of authority within a culture.

As you observe what is occurring in our society, are you seeing clear signs of secularism, humanism, and relativism? As these popular philosophies affect human thought and behavior, other closely related mindsets begin to surface. One step leads to another. One belief system opens the way to another way of thinking. Thus, we must

Recognize the Destructive Power of PLURALISM

God is moved out through secularism. Humans are moved in through humanism. And the philosophy of relativism means that there is no truth that is universal and binding. Is it any wonder that when these philosophies are shaping a culture, you would find the existence of another popular way of thinking called pluralism?

Pluralism is the idea that all points of view should be respected and tolerated. All beliefs and lifestyles are of equal value so long as those who embrace them are happy or on the way to happiness. The correct definition of tolerance—one that Christians can and should embrace—is that we should be willing to listen to everyone's point of view. It cannot mean that we are to automatically accept all points of view. Ravi Zacharias has correctly observed, "Truth cannot be sacrificed at the altar of pretended tolerance. Real tolerance is deference to all ideas, not indifference to the truth."

Under the banner of pluralism, the flag of truth and the flag of falsehood stand side by side, and their coexistence is applauded in the name of diversity.

Pluralism is the idea that every man has the right to believe anything he wishes to believe and become anything he wishes to become. However, this individual must not reach the point where he feels that what he believes and has become are what others should believe and become. In other words, a man should keep his convictions private. Pluralists become very intolerant of anyone who is intolerant. They say, "Everyone must bend so we can all blend."

We can easily see this philosophy at work in today's culture. It demands that our base of tolerance and acceptance be broad and all-inclusive. Because there are no absolutes, this means that no revelation, no Bible, and no authoritative system gives anyone the right to say that something is right or wrong for another person. Under the reign of modern-day pluralism, all gods must be given equal honor, and all beliefs deserve equal respect.

Secularism. Humanism. Relativism. Pluralism. There's a flow here. And, this points to another evil human philosophy that will be defined. We must also

Recognize the Destructive Power of NARCISSISM

Our English word "narcissism" is rooted in a story of Greek mythology. Narcissis was a handsome and stately youth of Greek legend that was content to sit incessantly and stare at his own reflection in a pool of water. Every day, he spent his life sitting and staring at himself. Obviously, the philosophy of narcissism is the practice of excessive self-love and self-gratification. So easily, humans can fall into the practice of "self-worship" (2 Timothy 3:2).

The natural tendency within the human heart (the Bible calls it "the sinful nature") is to reject the authority of God and practice autonomy or self-rule. It's the idea that "it's all about me."

> Those who live according to the sinful nature have their minds set on what that nature desires; but those who live in accordance with the Spirit have their minds set on what the Spirit desires. The mind of sinful man is death, but the mind controlled by the Spirit is life and peace; the sinful mind is hostile to God. It does not submit to God's law, nor can it do so. Those controlled by the sinful nature cannot please God (Romans 8:5-8).

When the spirit of narcissism reigns in a life, other behaviors are predictable. Are we seeing the sequential flow in these philosophies that are shaping this world? This flow points to one final human philosophy that will be defined. We must

Recognize the Destructive Power of HEDONISM

The Greek word *hedone* means pleasure. From this word, we get our word "hedonism." The hedonistic philosophy promotes the idea that human pleasure and sensuous enjoyments are the primary goals of life. Pleasure in this world is the chief objective. Thus, for the hedonist, every effort is made to enhance pleasure and mirth. You only live once; so go for it!

At least two types of hedonism are practiced. First, there is egotistic hedonism which promotes the idea that the individual should act out in whatever way will yield the maximum personal pleasure for the moment. "Do your own thing." "If it feels good, do it!" Second, there is a form of hedonism that has more of a utilitarian application. This hedonist is not so driven by the desire for personal pleasure but is focused more on promoting pleasure for the greatest number of people. The rightness or wrongness of any belief or behavior is measured by the amount of pleasure or displeasure that particular belief or behavior will bring to the people being affected. Thus, whatever action will bring the most pleasure to the most people becomes the right thing to do. Hedonism is a powerful force in today's culture.

This is interesting. In this short journey of pinpointing popular philosophies that are shaping our culture, a natural progression occurs. As the forces of secularism and humanism remove God from His throne, humans are quick to assume that throne and take the place of preeminence and honor.

> They exchanged the truth of God for a lie, and worshiped and served created things rather than the Creator—who is forever praised. Amen (Romans 1:25).

Dissemination of These Philosophies in the Culture

How does a culture that has strong Judeo-Christian influences and underpinnings become a culture that is saturated with such damaging and deadly influences? How does it happen? Desensitization occurs slowly over a long period of time through continuous exposure in small doses. Repetition. Repetition. Repetition. Teach the philosophy in the schools and institutions of higher learning. Air it through the media. Say it through cultural heroes. Embed it in the entertainment. Build it into the legal system. Promote it in the homes. At first, people are shocked when they hear something different; but after continuous exposure in small doses, they learn to tolerate it and quit fighting. Ultimately, what was once abnormal and unacceptable becomes normal and acceptable—even approved.

> They have become filled with every kind of wickedness, evil, greed and depravity. They are full of envy, murder, strife, deceit and malice. They are gossips, slanderers, God-haters, insolent, arrogant and boastful; they invent ways of doing evil; they disobey their parents; they are senseless, faithless,

heartless, ruthless. Although they know God's righteous decree that those who do such things deserve death, they not only continue to do these very things but also approve of those who practice them (Romans 1:29-32).

The Cumulative Effect on the Culture over the Years

These philosophies, along with others not mentioned, have had a cumulative effect on our culture over many years. A climate of unbelief creates a culture of corruption. Some are saying that we are now living in a post-Christian era. Many are calling our age a postmodern culture. The meaning of this label is that because long-standing beliefs and values of the modern age have failed us, we now have moved, philosophically, into a postmodern way of thinking. Postmodernists question everything. Biblical documents are not viewed as being reliable. A man's truth is nothing more than his opinion—merely the way he sees it from his vantage point. A more detailed description of postmodernism will be provided in chapter 10.

In a very real sense, the human philosophies mentioned above take us back to the sad events that occurred in the Garden of Eden with Adam and Eve. When Satan asked them the question, "Did God really say...?" the doorway was opened for the entry of secularism, humanism, relativism, pluralism, narcissism, hedonism, and even postmodernism. None of these philosophies are really new—even the spirit of postmodernism is as old as humankind. These ideologies have been at work for ages, and they, no doubt, will continue to be the preferred guidelines of those who choose to be self-ruled rather than God-ruled. In this modern age, the most independent human being that is opting for his way over God's way is actually walking in the footsteps of his or her original ancestors, Adam and Eve.

How Are Christians to Relate in Today's Culture?

As citizens of heaven, our minds are to be trained to be very sensitive to the will of God and the spirit of Jesus. Christianity is a healthy form of mind control (Matthew 28:18-20; 2 Corinthians 10:5).

Do not conform any longer to the pattern of this world, but be transformed by the renewing of your mind. Then you will be able to test and approve what God's will is—his good, pleasing and perfect will (Romans 12:2).

You, however, did not come to know Christ that way. Surely you heard of Him and were taught in Him in accordance with the truth that is in Jesus. You were taught, with regard to your former way of life, to put off your old self, which is being corrupted by its deceitful desires; to be made new in the attitude of your minds; and to put on the new self, created to be like God in true righteousness and holiness (Ephesians 4:20-24).

See to it that no one takes you captive through hollow and deceptive philosophy, which depends on human tradition and the basic principles of this world rather than on Christ (Colossians 2:8).

Citizens of heaven must continue to believe in and respect the Bible as the inspired Word of God. We believe that God has spoken in Scripture and that we can know and understand the truth that is essential to life in Jesus Christ. We must not seek to be absolute where God has not clearly commanded. We must not be meanspirited as we deal with others who have a different point of view. But with conviction and courage, we must stand firm for the truth revealed by God in the Bible.

from infancy you have known the Holy Scriptures, which are able to make you wise for salvation through faith in Christ Jesus. All Scripture is God-breathed and is useful for teaching, rebuking, correcting and training in righteousness, so that the man of God may be thoroughly equipped for every good work (2 Timothy 3:15-17).

Now the Bereans were of more noble character than the Thessalonians, for they received the message with great eagerness and examined the Scriptures every day to see if what Paul said was true (Acts 17:11).

FOR FURTHER DISCUSSION AND INTERACTION

1 How practical and helpful has it been to be reminded of these popular human philosophies that are shaping the culture of our day? How will an understanding of this material help you to live as a citizen of heaven in the midst of the culture of earth?

2 How cognizant do you think the average Christian is of the presence and power of these dominant philosophies? Among believers, what percentage do you estimate are aware of these evil tactics that the enemy is using to damage and destroy human lives?

3 If you have not already done so, go back to Ephesians 4:17-19 and trace the specific steps that Paul mentions as he pinpoints the human journey into sinful living. If possible, post these downward steps visually so that everyone can see and discuss their progressive nature.

4 Can you cite an actual experience in your own life to illustrate the presence of secularism? When? Where? Who? What? Why?

5 Do you agree or disagree with the observation made in this chapter that secularism is the umbrella philosophy of our day? Why?

6 It seems obvious that many in the secular world desire to be self-ruled rather than God-ruled. What is it about our sinful nature that makes this attractive and appealing?

7 Can you share an experience—yours or someone else's—where the practice of biblical truth has led to ridicule, rejection, or some other form of persecution?

8 Do you agree or disagree with the observation that none of the dominant philosophies mentioned in this chapter are actually new? Explain.

9 As you observe the movement of today's culture, how do you see the enemy disseminating the evil philosophies mentioned in this chapter and others? Has the process moved beyond the subtle stage? How can you protect yourself and those with whom you have influence from the toxic effects of such beliefs and behaviors?

10 How important is it for Christians in our day to study and know the Scriptures? How strong, in this respect, is the average believer today? What can and should we do to make improvements?

CITIZENS OF HEAVEN—RESIDENTS OF EARTH

CHAPTER 5

Be Submissive—Citizenship Recognizes Heaven's Jurisdiction

The King and His Monarchy

Jesus never invited sinners to enter the democracy of heaven. He did call them to repent and enter the kingdom of God (Mark 1:14, 15). Followers of Jesus hold primary citizenship in heaven and are members of a monarchy where He reigns continually as King and never has to run for re-election. While living as citizens in this heavenly monarchy, we also serve as citizens of an earthly democracy where the voice of the people is heard through elected representatives.

Simultaneously, we function in two very different spheres. In the monarchy, we submit to one supreme Ruler who has "[a]ll authority in heaven and on earth" and we pray for His kingdom to come and for His will to be done on earth as it is done in heaven (Matthew 6:9, 10; 28:18-20). In the democracy, we submit to the rule of the majority. But in all matters, the voice of the King in heaven has supremacy over the voice of the people on earth.

> Having brought the apostles, they made them appear before the Sanhedrin to be questioned by the high priest. "We gave you strict orders not to teach in this name," he said. "Yet you have filled Jerusalem with your teaching and are determined to make us guilty of this man's blood." Peter and the other apostles replied: "We must obey God rather than men!" (Acts 5:27-29).

> And He is the head of the body, the church; He is the beginning and the firstborn from among the dead, so that in everything He might have the supremacy (Colossians 1:18).

Transitioning from Democracy to Monarchy Is Not Easy

Many of us cut our teeth in an environment where secularistic humanism filled the air—and we inhaled. We have lived in a democracy where every person has a vote and a voice—we've always had our rights. Self-expression is a big thing in a free society. What a transition for us when, as followers of Jesus, our primary citizenship is transferred from a democracy to a monarchy. This can lead to major culture shock!

Under the reign of King Jesus, we have no vote or voice when it comes to matters of eternal salvation. His word is final. When I was in charge, the question was, "What do I want to do to be saved?" When I came to understand the truth of His lordship, the question became, "Lord, what would You have me do to be saved?" When God speaks in His Word and clearly tells us what is right, we have no right to believe otherwise and decide to modify what He has instructed us to do. His lordship always trumps our liberty.

> So we make it our goal to please Him, whether we are at home in the body or away from it (2 Corinthians 5:9).

To leave the pre-Christian environment where self-expression is celebrated and enter a Christian environment where self-expression is restricted is a huge transition for any person. Many people in our culture have existed for many years in a culture that likes having God around as long as He stays in His place and does not tell us how to think or what to do. Thus, it is not easy to live each day with a kingdom of God mindset which honors and submits to the jurisdiction of heaven.

> Then Jesus came to them and said, "All authority in heaven and on earth has been given to me. Therefore go and make disciples of all nations, baptizing them in the name of the Father and of the Son and of the Holy Spirit, and teaching them to obey everything I have commanded you. And surely I am with you always, to the very end of the age" (Matthew 28:18-20).

> Not everyone who says to me, "Lord, Lord," will enter the kingdom of heaven, but only he who does the will of my Father who is in heaven. Many will say to me on that day, "Lord, Lord, did we not prophesy in your name, and in your name drive out demons and perform many miracles?" Then I will tell them plainly, "I never knew you. Away from me, you evildoers!" (Matthew 7:21-23).

Communicating the Commands of the King

As it was during the days of Jesus' teaching ministry on earth, some today are shocked—even offended—if a teacher of the Bible lovingly refers to the clear commands of King Jesus as binding principles of truth for everyone (Matthew 7:28, 29). People are shocked at such political incorrectness. The spirit of relativism has conditioned many to believe that truth is unknown and unknowable. Doctrinal boldness—even when expressed with love and tenderness—is not in vogue. It is more acceptable to be vague. To stand firm on the basis of what the Bible teaches in the midst of a society of unbelief can result in a person being labeled as an ignorant, bigoted, right-winged, Bible-thumping fundamentalist. Yet the message of our King must be faithfully delivered!

Even some believers are uncomfortable if the Christian message is declared with clarity and conviction. They react negatively to such teaching and quickly dismiss it as legalistic. Legalism is abhorrent. It must be labeled, resisted, and eliminated from the colony of heaven. Teachers of the Word must be so careful to present the message in a Christ-exalting manner—with love—and never exude a spirit of self-righteousness. However, cheerful obedience to the clear commands of our Lord and King is not legalism. In fact, Jesus labeled such a response as love and a sure sign of friendship with Him.

> If you love me, you will obey what I command . . . Whoever has my commands and obeys them, he is the one who loves me. He who loves me will be loved by my Father, and I too will love him and show myself to him (John 14:15, 21).

> Jesus replied, "If anyone loves me, he will obey my teaching. My Father will love him, and we will come to him and make our home with him. He who does not love me will not obey my teaching. These words you hear are not my own; they belong to the Father who sent me" (John 14:23, 24).

> I will not speak with you much longer, for the prince of this world is coming. He has no hold on me, but the world must learn that I love the Father and that I do exactly what my Father has commanded me (John 14:30, 31).

> You are my friends if you do what I command (John 15:14).

Citizens of Heaven Have a High View of the Bible

As children, many of us sang the song, "Jesus Loves Me." The simple words of this familiar song speak volumes about the way the Bible is to be viewed. Recall those familiar lyrics, "Jesus loves me, this I know; for the Bible tells me so." What a healthy and holy view to instill in the hearts of little children. Yet this same submissive spirit is to live on in the lives of adults who are members of the colony of heaven. This is the attitude with which we view and approach the Bible. If the Bible says it's so, it's so!

With conviction and deep respect, we accept the Bible as the inspired, inerrant, and authoritative Word of God. It is important that we look at these three descriptive words up close.

The Bible Is INSPIRED

The inspiration of the Bible refers to the supernatural action of God upon the writers of the original manuscripts of the Scriptures. As they wrote, God was breathing His message into them, while at the same time allowing them to convey the message through their own writing styles and personalities. This inspired and God-guided message has been preserved in the Bible and provides for the human family the essential facts of history, the principles of truth, and the actions and commands of God.

> [A]nd how from infancy you have known the holy Scriptures, which are able to make you wise for salvation through faith in Christ Jesus. All Scripture is God-breathed and is useful for teaching, rebuking, correcting and training in righteousness, so that the man of God may be thoroughly equipped for every good work (2 Timothy 3:15-17).

> I want you to know, brothers, that the gospel I preached is not something that man made up. I did not receive it from any man, nor was I taught it; rather, I received it by revelation from Jesus Christ (Galatians 1:11, 12).

The Bible Is INERRANT

When all of the facts are known and properly understood, the Scriptures are completely true and accurate in content. This applies to doctrine, history, geography, science, and all other areas. The issue of inerrancy is a crucial dividing line that separates those who hold a "high view" of the Bible from those who do not. To deny the inerrancy of the Bible is to play loosely with the text of God's Word.

> I [Jesus[have much more to say to you [apostles], more than you can now bear. But when he, the Spirit of truth, comes, he will guide you into all truth. He will not speak on his own; he will speak only what he hears, and he will tell you what is yet to come. He will bring glory to me by taking from what is mine and making it known to you. All that belongs to the Father is mine. That is why I said the Spirit will take from what is mine and make it known to you (John 16:12-15).

> And we have the word of the prophets made more certain, and you will do well to pay attention to it, as to a light shining in a dark place, until the day dawns and the morning star rises in your hearts. Above all, you must understand that no prophecy of Scripture came about by the prophet's own interpretation. For prophecy never had its origin in the will of man, but men spoke from God as they were carried along by the Holy Spirit (2 Peter 1:19-21).

The Bible Is AUTHORITATIVE

Because the Bible is inspired and inerrant, it is authoritative. A fierce battle is being waged in today's world over the authority of the Bible. Many are openly declaring that the Bible has no authority whatsoever. Others want to straddle the fence and contend that the Bible has some authority depending on how you read and interpret it. But citizens of heaven demonstrate a heavenly wisdom by accepting and putting into practice the principles and truths taught by Jesus and communicated in the Scriptures.

> Therefore everyone who hears these words of mine and puts them into practice is like a wise man who built his house on the rock. The rain came down, the streams rose, and the winds blew and beat against that house; yet it did not fall, because it had its foundation on the rock. But everyone who hears these words of mine and does not put them into practice is like a foolish man who built his house on sand. The rain came down, the streams rose, and the winds blew and beat against that house, and it fell with a great crash (Matthew 7:24-29).

> As for the person who hears my words but does not keep them, I do not judge him. For I did not come to judge the world, but to save it. There is a judge for the one who rejects me and does not accept my words; that very word which I spoke will condemn him at the last day. For I did not speak of my own accord, but the Father who sent me commanded me what to say and how to say it (John 12:47-49).

Anchored to the Rock of God's Word

In an effort to make the Bible more appealing and acceptable to the masses, many have asked, "How can we modify the Bible so that it harmonizes with many of the popular ideas and values of this secular and scientific world?" Some want to be Christians, but just as strongly they want to be "with it." While professing that they wish to be anchored to the Rock, their actions would indicate that there is a deeper desire to be geared to the times.

The argument is that portions of the Bible are archaic and antiquated, which makes it impossible for intelligent people in the modern age to believe it. Therefore, we must "demythologize" (de-myth) the Bible. In fact, many of those who hold this view would say that the person who advocates accepting every part of the Bible as being truthful, historical, and accurate is its greatest enemy. They contend that such a narrow view repels large numbers of enlightened people because it puts them in the embarrassing position of having to embrace a faith that is rooted in ignorance and based on claims that cannot be verified scientifically.

Though many ridicule and criticize, citizens of heaven live cheerfully under the jurisdiction of heaven by remaining true to the Book that has stood as an unbreakable anvil through the centuries of time—the Bible. Critics come and go. The Bible stands. Opinions rise and fall. The Bible stands. Theories are declared and then renounced. The Bible stands.

By choice, we remain anchored to the rock of God's Word. Being geared to the times is important, but not paramount. For us, "The fear of the LORD is the beginning of knowledge" (Proverb 1:7). Our solid base is a healthy fear of God and a deep respect for His Word. This is where true knowledge begins. And from this beginning point, we never wish to be detached.

> Although I hope to come to you soon, I am writing you these instructions so that, if I am delayed, you will know how people ought to conduct themselves in God's household, which is the church of the living God, the pillar and foundation of the truth (1 Timothy 3:14, 15).

The Ranking Voice of Authority—My Voice? Our Voice? His Voice?

Across the land, there are numerous voices claiming the authority to enlighten and inform human beings of what is true and false, what is right and wrong, and what is acceptable and unacceptable. It is not difficult to see that these, so-called, voices of authority are conflicted—what one okays, another KO's.

> Woe to those who call evil good and good evil, who put darkness for light and light for darkness, who put bitter for sweet and sweet for bitter (Isaiah 5:20).

Thus, there is moral ambivalence in society and many have no clear idea of how one is to discern good from evil. However, citizens of heaven remain attuned to the clear voice of their Shepherd, Jesus. "[H]is sheep follow him because they know his voice" (John 10:4, 14-16). We have a choice as to which voice of authority will provide for us a solid base for our beliefs and behaviors. Which voice will you respect and heed as the highest-ranking authority for your life?

WILL I LISTEN TO "MY VOICE"?

"My voice" speaks within me and declares that I am a free and independent person. As such, I have the right to be self-ruled. I will be in control of my life; because ultimately, I am accountable to myself. Therefore, on the basis of what I believe in my heart to be right and best for me, I will order and direct the course of my life.

WILL I LISTEN TO "OUR VOICE"?

Think of "our voice" as the rule of civil law within our country. By submitting to the law of the land, I pledge to be controlled by the voice of the ruling majority. Within the moral and legal boundaries decided by a consensus of my fellow citizens on earth, I am free to believe and act. When our voice is viewed as one's highest source of authority, then the highest-ranking opinion would come from the nine justices of the U.S. Supreme Court. If this high court declares a certain belief or behavior to be legal, the matter is settled—unless the decision of the court is rescinded. There is no higher authority to which I must submit.

WILL I LISTEN TO "HIS VOICE"?

"His voice" refers to the supreme rule of God. As God, He claims all authority in heaven and on earth. No other voice, however confident or compelling, can equal or surpass His voice. The voice of the Father in heaven will always override "my voice" and "our voice" on earth. With this spirit of submission, I am enabled to open the Bible and read it obediently as the inspired, inerrant, and authoritative Word of God (1 Thessalonians 2:13; 2 Thessalonians 2:13-15) His voice always, in every situation, and on every issue dominates and overrules every other voice that speaks. For citizens of heaven, His voice is the final answer. When God speaks through His Word, the case is closed!

FOR FURTHER DISCUSSION AND INTERACTION

1 How difficult do you think it is for humans who have lived and functioned for years in a democracy to adjust to and accept the terms of life in a monarchy—the kingdom of heaven? At what point does the pain and difficulty of this transition begin to show?

2 How crucial and essential is it for a person to fully accept the lordship of Jesus Christ if he or she is to be a Christian? Are the terms of membership in the kingdom of God negotiable? In your discussion, refer to such passages as John 14:6, Acts 4:12, and Ephesians 4:4-6.

3 How could the concepts of this chapter be offensive to the unbeliever? How might the unbeliever respond to such teaching? In what sense could these concepts be refreshing and appealing to an unbeliever?

4 Based on the material in this chapter and other ideas that you can offer, attempt to distinguish between teaching that is truly legalistic and teaching that calls for a careful obedience to the Lord's commands.

5 To what dangers and difficulties is a person exposed once he or she embraces the view that the Bible contains errors and mistakes?

6 Do you see a difference in these two statements—"The Bible is the Word of God," and "The Bible contains the word of God"? How do these statements reflect some of the different points of view in our culture regarding the Bible?

7 What is our responsibility as far as presenting the message of the Bible in a society where many are doubtful? What can we do to make the message more appealing and inviting to the unbeliever? What are our limitations in this area?

8 Can you cite specific beliefs and behaviors that human authorities on earth have legalized which are forbidden by God's heavenly authority as revealed in the Bible?

9 How does the overall message of this chapter make you feel as a believer? Glad? Sad? Burdened? Freed? Threatened? Protected? As you are willing, share the reasons for your feelings.

10 Discuss the blessings and benefits that are experienced by citizens of heaven when they cheerfully make the choice to live obedient lives.

CHAPTER 6

Be Aware—Citizenship Calls for Discipleship and Disciplines (Part 1)

The Meaning of Discipleship

A disciple is a devoted learner and obedient follower of a master or teacher. For emphasis, read those words again slowly and thoughtfully. Ponder each word carefully. Citizens of heaven are to live as disciples of Jesus during their earthly residency.

> To the Jews who had believed him, Jesus said, "If you hold to my teaching, you are really my disciples. Then you will know the truth, and the truth will set you free" (John 8:31, 32).

Devoted disciples of Jesus are eager to know the mind of their Teacher and ready to embrace the beliefs and behaviors of their Master. The work of discipling cannot occur so long as disciples maintain a mind of their own. The words, "Yes, but..." should never fall from the lips of a disciple of Jesus. The teachings of the Master must be obeyed even if the comfort and convenience of the disciple are jeopardized. Jesus said, "Why do you call me 'Lord, Lord,' and do not do what I say?" (Luke 6:46).

Only as we begin to grasp the radical nature of Christian discipleship can we understand the strong words that Jesus spoke to people who were considering His claims and weighing their options as disciples. As they were asking, "Should we or shouldn't we?" the Master said

> Anyone who loves his father or mother more than me is not worthy of me; anyone who loves his son or daughter more than me is not worthy of me; and anyone who does not take his cross and follow me is not worthy of me. Whoever finds his life will lose it, and whoever loses his life for my sake will find it (Matthew 10:37-39).

The Demands of Discipleship

Jesus never tried to gain disciples under false pretenses. He never asked people to go on a picnic. As He set forth the terms of discipleship, Jesus used two of the hardest words for people to deal with and accept. They are "deny" and "cross."

Then he called the crowd to him along with his disciples and said: "If any-one would come after me, he must deny himself and take up his cross and follow me. For whoever wants to save his life will lose it, but whoever loses his life for me and for the Gospel will save it (Mark 8:34, 35).

The words "deny self" are not that difficult to understand, though difficult to practice. Denying self means saying "no" to oneself. As a disciple of Jesus, self-denial is not a one-time act, but a daily lifestyle and permanent mindset. This is made clear in Luke 9:23 where Jesus calls for daily cross bearing. His words were, "If anyone would come after me, he must deny himself and take up his cross daily and follow me." The martyr who gives his or her life in a heroic one-time act is to be greatly admired, but in some respects, it may be harder to die daily. Paul said, "I die every day" (1 Corinthians 15:31). True discipleship calls for a radical reorientation of life—with self no longer at the center.

"Take up your cross" are strong words that the serious disciple cannot superficially pass over. The first-century readers knew precisely what this meant. Most twenty-first-century readers know too, yet find ways to dilute the message. When the Roman Empire crucified a criminal, the victim was often forced to take up his cross and carry it to the place of execution. Thus, take up your cross can only mean a death to self. This phrase describes a de-liberate choice to do the will of God even if it means personal suffering, sac-rifice, or death—whatever the cost. In the game of baseball, we know what a sacrifice is. It's when a batter gives up his chance to get on base so another runner can advance or score. A sacrifice in the Old Testament was the offer-ing up of a valued animal or possession as a way of showing love for God. A sacrifice for us is to give up what we want or what we like so that we can be devoted to what God wants and likes.

The Impact of Discipleship

Discipleship means that a person willingly submits to a healthy form of mind control. To people whose hearts were tender and teachable, Jesus said, "Come to me, all you who are weary and burdened, and I will give you rest. Take my yoke upon you and learn from me, for I am gentle and humble in heart, and you will find rest for your souls. For my yoke is easy and my burden is light" (Matthew 11:28-30).

A commitment to follow Jesus involves a willingness to wear His easy yoke and carry His light burden. A yoke is a device of control. A voluntary acceptance of His yoke is an indication that a person is ready and willing for Jesus to be Lord and to have a controlling influence over his or her life. Under His control, the disciple gradually begins to resemble the Master—thinking, speaking, and behaving like Him.

Thus, maturing disciples of Jesus gradually come to have His mind and project His image (1 Corinthians 2:16). When outsiders observed the lifestyles of "first century disciples," their response was, "[T]hese men [have] been with Jesus" (Acts 4:13).

> Now the Lord is the Spirit, and where the Spirit of the Lord is, there is freedom. And we, who with unveiled faces all reflect the Lord's glory, are being transformed into his likeness with ever-increasing glory, which comes from the Lord, who is the Spirit (2 Corinthians 3:17, 18).

> My dear children, for whom I am again in the pains of childbirth until Christ is formed in you (Galatians 4:19).

The mind of Christ will produce the manner of Christ. Before sending His disciples out into the world to minister to others, He first called them into His presence so that they could know Him intimately. Effective discipleship today requires no less. We must come to Him before we are ready to go for Him.

> Jesus went up on a mountainside and called to him those he wanted, and they came to him. He appointed twelve—designating them apostles—that they might be with him and that he might send them out to preach (Mark 3:13, 14).

Have you been with Jesus? Do you know His mind and are you devoted to walking in His ways? Superficial religion, Sunday ritualism, and shallow church affiliation can never lead to the real and radical discipleship that is to characterize citizens of the kingdom of heaven. Discipleship is a process by which the will of God in heaven gradually becomes the way of man on earth. (Matthew 6:10).

Discipleship and Christian Discipline

Discipleship calls for discipline. Look at those words—"disciple" and "discipline." Even the spelling leads us to believe that they are related. A discipline is a consistent pattern of behavior taught to a disciple by his or her master. It is a fidelity and steadfastness to a certain course of action by which the disciple honors the teacher and heeds the teaching. Discipline evokes the idea of commitment, regimentation, and structure. It is a devotion to healthy habits, which reflect and reinforce the teachings of the master.

Christian disciplines encourage daily rhythms and life skills, which gradually result in the elimination of evil thoughts, harmful habits, and sinful speech. They provide the spiritual conduit through which God's power can flow into our lives so that we are gradually changed into the likeness of His

Son. These may be viewed as meaningful connections or appointments with God that gradually become healthy and wholesome habits.

The daily disciplines of the Christian life require daily discipline. The Christian patterns of life to which we committed yesterday must be repeated again today and then put into action again tomorrow if they are to accomplish their life-changing purposes.

Disciples who faithfully adhere to Christian disciplines are more likely to avoid the old ways of life that can hinder spiritual growth, and discover new pathways that keep them exposed to biblical truths, enriching ideas, faithful people, and constructive activities that nurture growth and development.

> Put to death, therefore, whatever belongs to your earthly nature: sexual immorality, impurity, lust, evil desires and greed, which is idolatry. Because of these, the wrath of God is coming. You used to walk in these ways, in the life you once lived. But now you must rid yourselves of all such things as these: anger, rage, malice, slander, and filthy language from your lips. Do not lie to each other, since you have taken off your old self with its practices and have put on the new self, which is being renewed in knowledge in the image of its Creator (Colossians 3:5-10).

It must be pointed out that as believers cultivate and practice daily spiritual disciplines, they are not earning or meriting favor and fellowship with God. Rather, they are putting into place a spiritual infrastructure through which God can supply food and fuel for Christ-like growth and development.

> Therefore, my dear friends, as you have always obeyed—not only in my presence, but now much more in my absence—continue to work out your salvation with fear and trembling, for it is God who works in you to will and to act according to his good purpose (Philippians 2:12, 13).

The Disciplines of Devoted Disciples—Acts 2:42

There is no one exhaustive list of Christian disciplines provided in the Scriptures. Some disciplines are commanded and must be practiced consistently by all believers at all times. Others are matters of choice and will be exercised at different times and in various ways by followers of Christ. As a person's relationship with the Lord deepens, there will be a variety of spiritual disciplines—life patterns—that will become a vital part of one's daily lifestyle.

There is, however, a key passage in Acts 2:42 which seems to provide a helpful model that summarizes some of the primary Christian disciplines of the early disciples and those that believers of all time are to pursue and practice. This passage pinpoints four distinct areas of Christian discipline to which God wants His people to be devoted. These four disciplines will be probed in some depth in this chapter and the two that follow it. Luke writes

> ## ACTS 2:42
>
> *They* [disciples of Jesus] DEVOTED THEMSELVES *to...*
> the Apostles' teaching
> *and to* the fellowship,
> *to* the breaking of bread
> *and* to prayer.

These life patterns and practices were priorities of God for His church. The Greek word translated devoted means an unrelenting adherence or commitment to something. Just because a person is involved in an activity does not necessarily mean that he or she is devoted to it. This passage provides helpful insight into what a devoted follower of Jesus looks like.

Because these were spiritual disciplines that fostered healthy and helpful life patterns for disciples in the first century, we can be assured that they will have the same impact on disciples in the twenty-first century. Devotion in these four areas of Christian discipline will greatly enhance the possibilities and probabilities for spiritual growth and maturity. We are now ready to explore the reasons as to why God desires for citizens of heaven to be "devoted to the apostles' teaching, and to the fellowship, to the breaking of bread and to prayer" (Acts 2:42).

1 DISCIPLES OF JESUS MUST BE DEVOTED TO THE APOSTLES' TEACHING.

That Word—Doctrine

The King James translation of Acts 2:42 has the words, "And they continued steadfastly in the apostles' doctrine . . . ." The new Christians in Jerusalem were devoted to doctrine.

In our pluralistic and post-modern culture, the word "doctrine" is a word that is resisted—even hated—by many who advocate a kind of tolerance that regards all beliefs, values, and lifestyles as equally valid. To these individuals, the word "doctrine" tends to connote a spirit of dogmatism and exclusiveness. For them, the most undesirable position for a person to embrace is "to know something and know that you know it." The proponents of tolerance can be very intolerant of people who believe that certain beliefs and behaviors are right and that other beliefs and behaviors are wrong for all people and for all time. They downplay the importance of doctrine and consider it to be irrelevant and marginal.

The Greek word used by Luke in Acts 2:42 is *didache* which means doctrine or teaching. The early disciples had no problem with the apostles' doctrine—in fact, they were devoted to it as we should be. To study and learn the teachings of the Bible is to study and learn the doctrines of Scripture. "Doctrine" is a good word—a biblical word that needs to be cleaned up and put back in circulation. Doctrine is important. Doctrine does matter. The doctrines of the Christian faith are the foundation blocks upon which the Christian life is built. Only as the doctrinal foundation remains strong and solid will the church of Jesus Christ have structural integrity.

> Consequently, you are no longer foreigners and aliens, but fellow citizens with God's people and members of God's household, built on the foundation of the apostles and prophets, with Christ Jesus himself as the chief cornerstone (Ephesians 2:19, 20).

> There is one body and one Spirit—just as you were called to one hope when you were called—one Lord, one faith, one baptism; one God and Father of all, who is over all and through all and in all (Ephesians 4:4-6).

The Apostles' Doctrine Is the Truth of God

The Christians described in Acts 2:42 did not merely engage in self-reflection as their avenue for discovering God's truth. Their motto was not, "Just follow your heart—go with your feelings." Their meetings were not occasions where everybody could put their own spin and interpretation on the teachings of the apostles. Instead, these disciples were devoted to the apostles' doctrine. The questions were not, "What will make me feel good?" or "What will our culture accept?" or "What will our long-standing religious traditions allow?" No! The question was, "What is God saying to us through His apostles and prophets?" They wanted to understand and practice the doctrine of the apostles. No one had the authority to act as editor-in-chief of the apostles' words. When these inspired teachers delivered their oral or written messages, faithful disciples were careful to listen, learn, and live out the truths that were taught.

> Surely you have heard about the administration of God's grace that was given to me for you, that is, the mystery made known to me by revelation, as I have already written briefly. In reading this, then, you will be able to understand my insight into the mystery of Christ, which was not made known to men in other generations as it has now been revealed by the Spirit to God's holy apostles and prophets (Ephesians 3:2-5).

And we also thank God continually because, when you received the word of God, which you heard from us, you accepted it not as the word of men, but as it actually is, the word of God, which is at work in you who believe (1 Thessalonians 2:13).

He called you to this through our gospel that you might share in the glory of our Lord Jesus Christ. So then, brothers, stand firm and hold to the teachings we passed on to you, whether by word of mouth or by letter (2 Thessalonians 2:14, 15).

In the presence of God and of Christ Jesus, who will judge the living and the dead, and in view of his appearing and his kingdom, I give you this charge: Preach the word; be prepared in season and out of season; correct, rebuke and encourage—with great patience and careful instruction. For the time will come when men will not put up with sound doctrine. Instead, to suit their own desires, they will gather around them a great number of teachers to say what their itching ears want to hear. They will turn their ears away from the truth and turn aside to myths. But you, keep your head in all situations, endure hardship, do the work of an evangelist, discharge all the duties of your ministry (2 Timothy 4:1-5).

Devoted disciples of Jesus in the early church craved the Word of God (1 Peter 2:1, 2). They read the Scriptures (1 Timothy 4:13). They were seekers of God's truth (Acts 10:33). They welcomed opportunities to meet with other believers and dig into the Word of God (Acts 11:25, 26). And when they heard the doctrines of the Christian faith presented, they were willing to obey (1 Thessalonians 2:13).

The Apostles' Doctrine Will Enable Us to Heal and Confront

Unless we know what the Bible teaches, we are ill equipped to deal effectively with the serious problems that weaken and destroy people's lives (2 Timothy 3:16, 17). Also, without an adequate knowledge of the Scriptures, we are unable to identify false doctrines and confront false teachers (Matthew 7:15-23). Modern-day Bereans are desperately needed. These were citizens of the city of Berea who welcomed Paul into their synagogue and allowed him to teach the Word of God. However, they were cautious, careful, and critical students as they listened to his message. They were devoted to the Word of God.

Now the Bereans were of more noble character than the Thessalonians, for they received the message with great eagerness and examined the Scriptures every day to see if what Paul said was true (Acts 17:11).

He [an elder, bishop, or pastor—all of these words refer to the same church leader] must hold firmly to the trustworthy message as it has been taught, so that he can encourage others by sound doctrine and refute those who oppose it (Titus 1:9).

The Apostles' Doctrine Will Provide a Biblical Worldview

A worldview is the lens or framework through which we view the world and attempt to make sense of what we see. Every person has a worldview. A worldview is any belief system, movement, religion, ideology, or philosophy that provides an authoritative set of beliefs for interpreting human experience and evaluating right and wrong.

Citizens of heaven must be ready, willing, and able to deliver to the residents of earth a message that deals with the issues of the day and is grounded in the truth of God's Word. Sadly, many in the secular culture are being taken captive by non-biblical ideas and behaviors. We must forge in our own lives and the lives of others a worldview that has deep roots in the Word of God. It is through devotion to the apostles' doctrine that this occurs. The goal is to develop a worldview that is based entirely on biblical truth, which is the essence of true Christian education.

We demolish arguments and every pretension that sets itself up against the knowledge of God, and we take captive every thought to make it obedient to Christ (2 Corinthians 10:5).

To Be Continued in Chapters 7 and 8

Our study of the four Christian disciplines listed in Acts 2:42 will be continued in the next two chapters. The three important disciplines that will be studied in Chapters 7 and 8 are devotion to the fellowship, devotion to the breaking of bread, and devotion to prayer.

FOR FURTHER DISCUSSION AND INTERACTION

1   After studying some of the teachings of Jesus on Christian discipleship, how would you compare His views with those of many in today's religious community? What can and should we be doing to close any gaps that may exist between Jesus' view of discipleship and ours? Do the terms of discipleship as stated by Christ in the first century still have meaning and relevancy for us today?

2   Do you agree with the assertion that discipleship in the kingdom of God involves a healthy form of mind control? What reaction do you think this might cause on the part of many people in today's culture?

3   Do you believe that most Christian teachers in today's world are stressing and emphasizing the importance of denying self and taking up one's cross daily? If not, why not?

4   Based on your own personal experience and what you observe in the lives of others, what percentage of believers today are living sacrificial Christian lives?

5   Jesus said, "For my yoke is easy and my burden is light" (Matthew 11:30). In what sense is Jesus' yoke easy and His burden light?

6   Share with others what you have learned about practicing Christian disciplines. What has worked for you? What has been the most difficult part of the process? What particular Christian discipline has been a blessing and boost to your spiritual development?

7   In this chapter, it was pointed out that many in today's religious world have an aversion to the word "doctrine." How do you view this word? Is doctrine important? Should we study and teach doctrine? Has the world's negative view of doctrine had an impact on the way believers view and treat doctrine? Explain your responses.

8   Frequently, we hear people speak about the importance of "following your heart" and "embracing what feels good." Are these safe and reliable guidelines as we seek to read and obey the Word of God? Explain.

9   Generally, do you believe that the Berean spirit (Acts 17:11) is alive and well in the church today? Elaborate on your answer.

10 Based on a scale of 0 (low) – 10 (high), how would you grade our present day efforts to instill a biblical worldview in the lives of those who are members of our families and churches?

CITIZENS OF HEAVEN—RESIDENTS OF EARTH

CHAPTER 7

Be Aware—Citizenship Calls for Discipleship and Disciplines (Part 2)

Christian Discipleship and the Disciplines

When Christian discipleship is taken seriously, Christian disciplines are practiced faithfully. A Christian discipline is a pattern of behavior that is implemented so consistently over a period of time that one's life is deeply affected. You engage in this spirit-building activity today. You repeat the practice tomorrow. You do it again. And again. At a certain point, the practice is more than something you do—it becomes a part of who you are. Someone said, "Practice does not necessarily make perfect, but it does make permanent." To practice Christian disciplines is to commit to lifestyle patterns that hone and shape your life so that Christlikeness is gradually created. There is a vital connection between Christian discipleship and the practice of Christian disciplines.

Some of the Disciplines of Devoted Disciples—Acts 2:42

As was pointed out in the previous chapter, Acts 2:42 provides a helpful model that summarizes some of the primary Christian disciplines of the early disciples, and those that believers of all time are to pursue and practice. This passage pinpoints four distinct areas of Christian discipline to which God wants His people to be devoted. Luke writes

ACTS 2:42

They [disciples of Jesus] DEVOTED THEMSELVES *to . . .*
the apostles' teaching
and to the fellowship,
to the breaking of bread
and to prayer.

In Chapter 6, the focus was on the early Christians' devotion to the apostles' doctrine. In Chapter 7, we will focus attention on the need for devotion to the fellowship, and the breaking of bread. In Chapter 8, the focus on

Christian disciplines will continue with a study on the believer's need to be devoted to prayer.

2 DISCIPLES OF JESUS MUST BE DEVOTED TO THE FELLOWSHIP.

"The Fellowship"—What Does This Mean?

The faith action that makes us one with Jesus Christ also unites us with His body, the church, and makes us one with each other. When I am joined to Him, at that same time, I am joined to you, my fellow Christian. This spiritual union of fellow believers in the Lord Jesus is called the fellowship.

> You are all sons of God through faith in Christ Jesus, for all of you who were baptized into Christ have clothed yourselves with Christ. There is neither Jew nor Greek, slave nor free, male nor female, for you are all one in Christ Jesus (Galatians 3:26-28).

This means that our saving union with Jesus opens the way for our sweet communion with each other. My union with Him creates a communion with you. The moment God becomes my Father, you become my brother or sister assuming you, too, are His child. And, together, we enter a fellowship and a partnership in which our lives are to be shared in meaningful and constructive ways. It was to this fellowship that the early Christians were devoted according to Acts 2:42.

The Greek word for fellowship is *koinonia*. This term is translated in several ways in the New Testament such as partnership (Luke 5:10), participation (1 Corinthians 10:16, 17), and sharing (Romans 12:13). The central idea is shared life. This means that Christian fellowship is more than social activities centered around food and fun. The fellowship is the presence of close and committed relationships between believers. It is the common bond that we enjoy together in the Holy Spirit. This spiritual bond continually prompts us to share our lives with one another and communicate at a deep level about matters that are very important.

> A new command I give you: Love one another. As I have loved you, so you must love one another. By this all men will know that you are my disciples, if you love one another (John 13:34, 35).

> The body is a unit, though it is made up of many parts; and though all its parts are many, they form one body. So it is with Christ. For we were all baptized by one Spirit into one body–whether Jews or Greeks, slave or free—and we were all given the one Spirit to drink (1 Corinthians 12:12, 13).

This is how we know what love is: Jesus Christ laid down his life for us. And we ought to lay down our lives for our brothers (1 John 3:16).

"The Fellowship" of Believers Is Unique

The fellowship that Christians experience can only be explained and experienced when supernatural realities are taken into account. When two unbelievers relate, the interaction is purely between two persons. However, when two believers enter into a relationship, there are actually three persons involved—God, and the two individuals who share mutual life as members of the body of Christ. This means when Christian fellowship is experienced, much more is going on than what appears on the surface. Fellowship between unbelievers is in the flesh. The fellowship between believers is in the Spirit.

> We proclaim to you what we ourselves have seen and heard, so that you also may have fellowship with us. And our fellowship is with the Father and with his Son, Jesus Christ (1 John 1:3).

> May the grace of the Lord Jesus Christ, and the love of God, and the fellowship of the Holy Spirit be with you all (2 Corinthians 13:14).

Nonbelievers who share membership in human organizations can have superficial fellowship while engaging in casual chitchat, exchanging pleasantries, nibbling on party refreshments, or sharing in some project or activity. Their unity is rooted in common interests, similar personalities, and shared points of view. Those who are outside the Christian community may never understand the intimacy that Christians enjoy as they share a oneness made possible by the Spirit of God. Believers can be very different in their personalities and preferences, yet still enjoy a beautiful spiritual unity in the Lord. As we connect and commune with the Lord and each other, there are supernatural forces at work, which we cannot see. Paul wrote, "So from now on, we regard no one from a wordly point of view" (2 Corinthians 5:16).

> If you have any encouragement from being united with Christ, if any comfort from his love, if any fellowship with the Spirit, if any tenderness and compassion, then make my joy complete by being like-minded, having the same love, being one in spirit and purpose. Do nothing out of selfish ambition or vain conceit, but in humility consider others better than yourselves. Each of you should look not only to your own interests, but also to the interests of others (Philippians 2:1-4).

Are you familiar with the words to the popular Christian song—"Sweet, Sweet Spirit"—written by Doris Akers? It truly describes the tone and tenor—the spirit—of the fellowship we enjoy in Jesus Christ.

Sweet Sweet Spirit

There's a sweet, sweet Spirit in this place,
And I know that it's the Spirit of the Lord.
There are sweet expressions on each face,
And I know they feel the presence of the Lord.

Sweet Holy Spirit, Sweet heavenly Dove,
Stay right here with us,
Filling us with Your love.
And for these blessings, we lift our hearts in praise,
Without a doubt we'll know that we have been revived,
When we shall leave this place.

The fellowship mentioned in Acts 2:42 is not experienced when bored and detached religious people sit passively through a weekly worship assembly of the church, while staring at the back of heads. Though their hands may connect with church greeters who are stationed at the exit doors, there may be absolutely no connection occurring at the heart level. In too many churches today, the scene resembles little more than what occurs when spectators gather in a local theater to watch the show and then hurry away to the privacy of their own worlds. For theatergoers, the goal is personal entertainment rather than meaningful interaction designed to nurture mutual spiritual growth. Assembling to merely watch the show can never suffice for the fellowship to which Christians are to be devoted.

Devotion to "The Fellowship" Means Mutual Concern and Real Caring

When citizens of God's family are devoted to the fellowship, a safe and secure environment is created. Every person is known, loved, needed, and valued. Genuine compassion is demonstrated in practical ways on a daily basis. If members are absent when the church assembles, they are missed and sought after. No one in the family circle needs to fear for his or her backside. It's one for all and all for one. If one member suffers, all members suffer. If one member is rejoicing, all members rejoice. The goal is to complete each other—not compete with each other. Efforts are made to build each other up—not tear each other down. The fellowship is to be a circle of love where fellow believers are prayed for and not preyed upon.

> All the believers were together and had everything in common. Selling their possessions and goods, they gave to anyone as he had need (Acts 2:44, 45).

> Be devoted to one another in brotherly love. Honor one another above yourselves (Romans 12:10).

> Share with God's people who are in need. Practice hospitality (Romans 12:13).

> Rejoice with those who rejoice; mourn with those who mourn. Live in harmony with one another. Do not be proud, but be willing to associate with people of low position. Do not be conceited (Romans 12:15, 16).

> so that there should be no division in the body, but that its parts should have equal concern for each other. If one part suffers, every part suffers with it; if one part is honored, every part rejoices with it (1 Corinthians 12:25, 26).

Devotion to "The Fellowship" Means Obedience to the "One Anothering" Passages

In some ways, the Christian life is very personal—even private. It involves a beautiful relationship between one God and one person. However, if a believer is to enjoy the fullness and richness of the Christian lifestyle, there must be meaningful and significant interaction with others. An individual's personal relationship with one God will inevitably lead to meaningful "one anothering" relationships with other believers within the fellowship.

In fact, there are many important aspects of the Christian life that can only occur when disciples are willing to share their lives with "one another at deep levels. This truth is confirmed when you consider the numerous one anothering" passages that appear in the New Testament documents. The following examples illustrate the point:

> Be devoted to one another (Romans 12:10)
> Honor one another (Romans 12:10; Philippians 2:3)
> Be like minded toward one another (Romans 12:16; 15:5)
> Edify one another (Romans 14:19; 1 Thessalonians 5:11)
> Accept one another (Romans 15:7)
> Admonish one another (Romans 15:14; Colossians 3:16)
> Greet one another (Romans 16:16; 1 Corinthians 16:20; 2 Corinthians 13:12)

Wait for one another (1 Corinthians 11:33)
Care for one another (1 Corinthians 12:25)
Serve one another (Galatians 5:13; 1 Peter 4:10)
Carry the burdens of one another (Galatians 6:2)
Bear with one another (Ephesians 4:2; Colossians 3:13)
Forgive one another (Ephesians 4:32; Colossians 3:13)
Be kind to one another (Ephesians 4:32; 1 Thessalonians 5:15)
Sing to one another (Ephesians 5:19; Colossians 3:16)
Submit to one another (Ephesians 5:21; 1 Peter 5:5)
Teach one another (Colossians 3:16)
Encourage one another (1 Thessalonians 4:18; 5:11; Hebrews 3:13; 10:25)
Spur on one another (Hebrews 10:24)
Confess faults to one another (James 5:16)
Pray for one another (James 5:16)
Be hospitable to one another (1 Peter 4:9)
Have fellowship with one another (1 John 1:7)

Obviously, these "one anothering" actions cannot exist in an environment where Christians live as isolated, detached, and independent persons. The Church is a body knit together (Colossians 2:19), and Christians are members of one another (Romans 12:5; Ephesians 4:25).

And let us consider how we may spur one another on toward love and good deeds. Let us not give up meeting together, as some are in the habit of doing, but let us encourage one another—and all the more as you see the Day approaching (Hebrews 10:24, 25).

Devotion to "The Fellowship" Means Accountability and Correction

When citizens of heaven are devoted to the fellowship, they cheerfully submit to each other in a spirit of mutual cooperation and dependency. Individual members are not to act as freelancers insisting on their personal rights to think, speak, and act without due regard for others within the community. If someone is involved in sinful or questionable behavior, members of the fellowship are to take loving action to bring about any changes that may be needed. This is corrective discipline that is necessary if a healthy kind of accountability is practiced.

I have written you in my letter not to associate with sexually immoral people—not at all meaning the people of this world who are immoral, or the greedy and swindlers, or idolaters. In that case you would have to leave this world. But now I am writing you that you must not associate with anyone who calls himself a brother but is sexually immoral or greedy, an idolater or a slanderer, a drunkard or a swindler. With such a man do not even eat (1 Corinthians 5:9-11).

Brothers, if someone is caught in a sin, you who are spiritual should restore him gently. But watch yourself, or you also may be tempted. Carry each other's burdens, and in this way you will fulfill the law of Christ (Galatians 6:1, 2).

For of this you can be sure: No immoral, impure or greedy person--such a man is an idolater--has any inheritance in the kingdom of Christ and of God. Let no one deceive you with empty words, for because of such things God's wrath comes on those who are disobedient. Therefore do not be partners with them (Ephesians 5:5-7).

Warn a divisive person once, and then warn him a second time. After that, have nothing to do with him (Titus 3:10).

Such actions call for tough love among believers. Though not easy, these disciplinary actions are necessary if the fellowship is to remain strong and pure (Matthew 5:23, 24; 18:15-17).

Devotion to "The Fellowship" Calls for Believers to Be Motivated and Equipped for Ministry

Each person within the fellowship has been given special abilities and talents from God—known as spiritual gifts. Every believer has at least one ministry gift or talent. There are no useless members of the body. Gifts are given for the common good of everyone. The goal is to build up the body rather than to selfishly promote oneself. In order for the body of Christ to function in a healthy and effective manner, it is essential that each member exercise his or her ministry gift in a cheerful and constructive manner.

Just as each of us has one body with many members, and these members do not all have the same function, so in Christ we who are many form one body, and each member belongs to all the others (Romans 12:4, 5).

Now the body is not made up of one part but of many. If the foot should say, "Because I am not a hand, I do not belong to the body," it would not for that reason cease to be part of the body. And if the ear should say, "Because I am not an eye, I do not belong to the body," it would not for that reason cease to be part of the body. If the whole body were an eye, where would the sense of hearing be? If the whole body were an ear, where would the sense of smell be? But in fact God has arranged the parts in the body, every one of them, just as he wanted them to be. If they were all one part, where would the body be? As it is, there are many parts, but one body. The eye cannot say to the hand, "I don't need you!" And the head cannot say to the feet, "I don't need you!" On the contrary, those parts of the body that seem to be weaker are indispensable, and the parts that we think are less honorable we treat with special honor. And the parts that are unpresentable are treated with special modesty, while our presentable parts need no special treatment. But God has combined the members of the body and has given greater honor to the parts that lacked it, so that there should be no division in the body, but that its parts should have equal concern for each other. If one part suffers, every part suffers with it; if one part is honored, every part rejoices with it. Now you are the Body of Christ, and each one of you is a part of it (1 Corinthians 12:14-27).

From him the whole body, joined and held together by every supporting ligament, grows and builds itself up in love, as each part does its work (Ephesians 4:16).

3 DISCIPLES OF JESUS MUST BE DEVOTED TO THE BREAKING OF BREAD.

Is There a Pattern in Acts 2:42?

When you study the four Christian disciplines mentioned in Acts 2:42, there seems to be an interesting pattern in the way they are ordered. The first and fourth disciplines—devotion to the apostles' doctrine and prayer—are interactions which are largely vertical in nature. Through the apostles' doctrine, God speaks to us. And, through prayer, we speak to God. Both are vertical interactions.

However, when you consider the second and third Christian disciplines mentioned in Acts 2:42—devotion to the fellowship and the breaking of bread—there are powerful horizontal dynamics at work in both cases. Let's probe the Christian discipline referred to as a devotion to breaking bread.

The Significance of Breaking Bread

What does it mean for citizens of heaven to be devoted to the breaking of bread? In our biological families, mealtimes should be opportunities for encouraging family unity and constructive communication. Sharing a meal together can be a wonderful time to discuss the events of the day or to share insights related to the meaning of life. In most cultures, the act of eating together is a universal sign of unity. Generally, we love the people we eat with. There is something significant about breaking bread together.

It is interesting to note that the word "companionship" stems from two Latin words—*cum* which means "with" and *panis* which means "bread." Thus, when combined to form the word "companionship," the literal meaning of this word is "with bread." Frequently, in the course of human events, a shared meal is a demonstration of unity and companionship. A meal eaten alone can seem like nothing more than the intake of food, whereas food that is eaten in a spirit of unity with people you love is considered a feast.

These same principles hold true for the family of God. For many people who lived in the first-century culture, mealtime was a sacred time—a time for giving thanks to God and sharing precious moments with people you love. Note the wording in Acts 2:46 where Luke describes the atmosphere that surrounded the breaking of bread that occurred in the first-century church.

> Every day they continued to meet together in the temple courts. They broke bread in their homes and ate together with glad and sincere hearts (Acts 2:46).

When you carefully study the wording of this verse, it is easy to see that there was something distinctive about these meals that were eaten in a spirit of joy and celebration. No doubt, some of the first-century believers could remember the wonderful times and memorable experiences they had shared with the Master while breaking bread together with Him. Each meal that they shared together would have been a vivid reminder of the One who had so often broken bread with His disciples during His earthly ministry.

When and Where Are Believers to Break Bread Together?

Clearly, we are to be devoted to breaking bread, but when and where does this kind of interaction occur within the Christian family?

First, we break bread when we assemble together on Sunday, the Lord's Day, to eat the Lord's Supper. During this observance, Christians commune with the Lord and each other. Toward the close of Paul's third missionary journey, he was hurrying to reach the city of Jerusalem by Pentecost (Acts 20:16). Yet in spite of this time crunch, Paul opted to delay his journey for several days so that he could eat the Lord's Supper with the Christians of Troas during their regular Sunday assembly. In Troas, this weekly assembly of believers is described as a matter of fact.

On the first day of the week, we came together to break bread. Paul spoke to the people and, because he intended to leave the next day, kept on talking until midnight (Acts 20:7).

A weekly coming together of believers is further suggested by the fact that in 1 Corinthians 16:1, 2, Paul instructed the Christians in Corinth, as he had similarly instructed the Galatian churches, to make an allocation of money every Sunday to assist with special needs. The implication is that the believers were assembling together each Sunday.

Now about the collection for God's people: Do what I told the Galatian churches to do. On the first day of every week, each one of you should set aside a sum of money in keeping with his income, saving it up, so that when I come no collections will have to be made (1 Corinthians 16:1, 2).

Furthermore, when you examine Paul's words to the church in Corinth, it is clear that they observed the Lord's Supper in conjunction with the sharing of a fellowship meal, which may have been referred to in those early days as an Agape/Love Feast (Jude 10; 2 Peter 2:13). It is reasonable to believe that the Agape Feast and the Lord's Supper were employed as interchangeable designations for the whole celebration known as communion.

In 1 Corinthians 11:17-34 Paul rebukes the Corinthians for their abuse of the Love Feast. Instead of a unity meal where love and acceptance were being practiced, the Corinthians were practicing a divisive spirit by enjoying private meals with members of their own cliques.

Paul commands them to correct these abuses by "wait[ing] for each other" (I Corinthians 11:33) so that "bread could be broken" in a spirit of Christian love and unity. Paul makes it clear that if believers "break bread"—eat their so-called "fellowship meal"—in a setting where division and sectarianism are being practiced, the true meaning of Christian communion is missed and the "Lord's Supper" is not observed (v. 20). The solution to the problem is for Christian believers to properly discern the body—recognize the oneness of the church (v. 29). And, to fail in this matter is to bring judgment upon oneself (v. 34).

In the following directives I have no praise for you, for your meetings do more harm than good. In the first place, I hear that when you come together as a church, there are divisions among you, and to some extent I believe it. No doubt there have to be differences among you to show which of you have God's approval. When you come together, it is not the Lord's Supper you eat, for as you eat, each of you goes ahead without waiting for anybody else. One remains hungry, another gets drunk. Don't you have homes to eat and drink in? Or do you despise the church of God and humiliate those who have nothing? What shall I say to you? Shall I praise you for this? Certainly not!

For I received from the Lord what I also passed on to you: The Lord Jesus, on the night He was betrayed, took bread, and when he had given thanks, he broke it and said, "This is my body, which is for you; do this in remembrance of me." In the same way, after supper he took the cup, saying, "This cup is the new covenant in my blood; do this, whenever you drink it, in remembrance of me." For whenever you eat this bread and drink this cup, you proclaim the Lord's death until he comes.

Therefore, whoever eats the bread or drinks the cup of the Lord in an unworthy manner will be guilty of sinning against the body and blood of the Lord. A man ought to examine himself before he eats of the bread and drinks of the cup. For anyone who eats and drinks without recognizing the body of the Lord eats and drinks judgment on himself. That is why many among you are weak and sick, and a number of you have fallen asleep. But if we judged ourselves, we would not come under judgment. When we are judged by the Lord, we are being disciplined so that we will not be condemned with the world.

So then, my brothers, when you come together to eat, wait for each other. If anyone is hungry, he should eat at home, so that when you meet together it may not result in judgment. And when I come I will give further directions (1 Corinthians 11:17-34).

Is not the cup of thanksgiving for which we give thanks a participation in the blood of Christ? And is not the bread that we break a participation in the body of Christ? Because there is one loaf, we, who are many, are one body, for we all partake of the one loaf (1 Corinthians 10:16, 17).

Second, Christians are to break bread at times other than during their Sunday assemblies. Sharing food is a wonderful way to promote communication and deepen relationships within the Christian family. In the early church, bread was broken in home settings. These gatherings occurred frequently—even daily. Meaningful fellowship was shared and the Word of God was read and taught. Bread for the stomach was served as the bread of life was shared by truth-seeking believers.

Every day they continued to meet together in the temple courts. They broke bread in their homes and ate together with glad and sincere hearts (Acts 2:46).

Day after day, in the temple courts and from house to house, they never stopped teaching and proclaiming the good news that Jesus is the Christ (Acts 5:42).

Certainly, in the earliest days of the church in Jerusalem, when many had converted to Christianity while on a pilgrimage to the city to observe Passover, there were special meals provided for those who lacked the necessities of life.

All the believers were one in heart and mind. No one claimed that any of his possessions was his own, but they shared everything they had. With great power the apostles continued to testify to the resurrection of the Lord Jesus, and much grace was upon them all. There were no needy persons among them. For from time to time those who owned lands or houses sold them, brought the money from the sales and put it at the apostles' feet, and it was distributed to anyone as he had need (Acts 4:32-35).

In Acts 6:1, Luke describes a daily distribution of food to needy widows that was occurring—bread was broken. It is easy to understand how all of these shared meals opened the way for believers to experience a spiritual bond that united them with each other and with the Lord. The meals were occasions for something greater and deeper than the mere distribution of food.

To Be Continued in Chapter 8

Our study of the four Christian disciplines listed in Acts 2:42 will be continued in the next chapter. The fourth important discipline that will be the focus of Chapter 8 is devotion to prayer.

FOR FURTHER DISCUSSION AND INTERACTION

1 Identify three factors that make it difficult for modern-day believers to be consistent and faithful in the practice of Christian disciplines.

2 Contrast the fellowship described in the New Testament with the understanding that most people in the religious world have of fellowship.

3 Can you point to a setting or relationship that you have experienced which comes closest to matching the fellowship as described in the New Testament? Would you be willing to share details of this experience with other believers?

4 What differences can you identify between the unity that exists within the membership of a civic club and the unity that Christians enjoy in the Lord?

5 How does the spirit of individualism and the desire for privacy within our culture affect our ability to actually be the fellowship as described in Acts 2:42?

6 It was mentioned in this chapter that some local churches can resemble the environment of a theater where people assemble to watch the show and then return to the privacy of their personal lives. How can we prevent and/or correct this problem and learn the true meaning of being devoted to the fellowship?

7 Looking at the list of "one anothering" passages listed in this chapter, identify one of these interactions that sounds especially appealing to you—one that you would like to experience more than you are at the present time.

8 In view of what the Scriptures teach about the fellowship, what fresh insights can you offer in connection with the importance of regular attendance to and participation in church assemblies?

9 Does the concept of the fellowship necessarily mean that there must be some kind of mutual accountability to each other? What areas of accountability do you believe are needed in most churches? What dangers must be avoided when the accountability principle is taught and practiced?

10 In the fellowship of which you are now a part, approximately what percentage of the members have a clear vision of their spiritual gifts and understand how those talents can and should be deployed in practical Christian ministry?

11 Describe the most meaningful experience of breaking bread that you experience in your life as a Christian. Give reasons as to why this particular experience is meaningful to you.

12 In view of the fact that breaking bread together is a sign of unity and oneness, discuss the implications that you see in the following passages: Psalm 41:9 (John 13:18-27); Mark 2:15, 16; Acts 16:13-15; Acts 16:25-34; Luke 15:11-24; Revelation 3:19, 20; and 1 Corinthians 5:9-11.

13 What steps can be taken to strengthen our Christian ministry in the home setting? Why are we not using our homes more effectively to strengthen the fellowship? Can you identify a particular home ministry where you, personally, have been strengthened and blessed as the gift of hospitality was practiced?

CHAPTER 8

Be Aware—Citizenship Calls for Discipleship and Disciplines (Part 3)

Disciplines of Devoted Disciples—Acts 2:42

As was pointed out in the two previous chapters, Acts 2:42 provides a helpful model that summarizes some of the primary Christian disciplines of the early disciples and those that believers of all time are to pursue and practice. If citizens of heaven who reside on earth are to keep their upward focus, these are disciplines that must be cultivated. This passage pinpoints four distinct areas of Christian discipline to which God wants His people to be devoted. Luke writes

ACTS 2:42

They [disciples of Jesus] DEVOTED THEMSELVES *to . . .*
the apostles' teaching
and to the fellowship,
to the breaking of bread
and **to** prayer.

In Chapters 6-7, the focus was on the early Christians' devotion to the apostles' doctrine, the fellowship, and the breaking of bread. In this chapter, the study of Christian disciplines will continue with a close-up look at the believer's need to be devoted to prayer.

4 DISCIPLES OF JESUS MUST BE DEVOTED TO PRAYER.

The Church Is to Be a House of Prayer

A few days before Jesus was crucified, He entered the temple area in Jerusalem and did some serious housecleaning.

Jesus entered the temple area and drove out all who were buying and selling there. He overturned the tables of the money changers and the benches of those selling doves. "It is written," he said to them, "My house will be called a house of prayer, but you are making it a den of robbers" (Matthew 21:12, 13).

Even while Jesus was driving the robbers out of the temple and putting His Father's house back in order, He was quoting passages from the Old Testament which made it clear that this was to be a place where people prayed—not a place where people would be preyed upon. Does God still have a temple or house in which He dwells, and if He does, is it still to be a house of prayer?

According to the Scriptures, God no longer lives in a physical temple built by human hands (Acts 7:48; 17:24). However, the Bible does refer to a temple or house in which He dwells even today. Christians are His temple—His house—and He lives personally within our hearts (1 Corinthians 3:16, 17; 2 Corinthians 6:16; Ephesians 2:19-22; Hebrews 3:5, 6). In beautiful symbolism, the Scriptures refer to Christians as "living stones" in the temple of God. And, yes! As God's temple, we are still to be a house of prayer.

> As you come to him, the living Stone—rejected by men but chosen by God and precious to him—you also, like living stones, are being built into a spiritual house to be a holy priesthood, offering spiritual sacrifices acceptable to God through Jesus Christ (I Peter 2:4, 5).

> But you are a chosen people, a royal priesthood, a holy nation, a people belonging to God, that you may declare the praises of him who called you out of darkness into his wonderful light (1 Peter 2: 9).

The Vital Role of Prayer in the Early Church

Even a cursory reading of the book of Acts makes it clear that these pioneers of the Christian faith prayed fervently and frequently. Clearly, these first-century believers were "devoted to prayer" (Acts 2:42). They were persistent and consistent as they cried out to God during the days of their pilgrimage on this earth. A few examples will demonstrate their devotion to prayer:

1 After Jesus ascended back to heaven, His followers waited expectantly in Jerusalem for the coming of the Holy Spirit. As they waited, they prayed.

Do not miss the significance of the praying that occurred in Acts 1. Too often, we have been so focused on the power that was poured out in Acts 2 that we have overlooked or forgotten the prayer that was offered up in Acts 1. Devotion to prayer in Acts 1 preceded the powerful evangelism that occurred in Acts 2.

When they arrived, they went upstairs to the room where they were staying. Those present were Peter, John, James and Andrew; Philip and Thomas, Bartholomew and Matthew; James son of Alphaeus and Simon the Zealot, and Judas son of James. They all joined together constantly in prayer, along with the women and Mary the mother of Jesus, and with his brothers (Acts 1:13, 14).

2 After the Spirit was poured out and the church was established in Jerusalem, the new converts to Christianity devoted themselves to prayer.

"Therefore let all Israel be assured of this: God has made this Jesus, whom you crucified, both Lord and Christ." When the people heard this, they were cut to the heart and said to Peter and the other apostles, "Brothers, what shall we do?" Peter replied, "Repent and be baptized, every one of you, in the name of Jesus Christ for the forgiveness of your sins. And you will receive the gift of the Holy Spirit" (Acts 2:36-38).

Those who accepted his message were baptized, and about three thousand were added to their number that day. They devoted themselves to the apostles' teaching and to the fellowship, to the breaking of bread and to prayer (Acts 2:41, 42).

3 When the enemies of Christianity made life difficult for the followers of Jesus and persecuted them because of their faith, these first-century disciples called out to God in prayer.

Frequently, the followers of Jesus were unfairly discriminated against, falsely accused, and brutally punished. Their opponents were filled with vitriol and violence. How did they cope? Amazingly, in the midst of such horrible conditions, they continued to pray and sing.

When the owners of the slave girl realized that their hope of making money was gone, they seized Paul and Silas and dragged them into the marketplace to face the authorities. They brought them before the magistrates and said, "These men are Jews, and are throwing our city into an uproar by advocating customs unlawful for us Romans to accept or practice." The crowd joined in the attack against Paul and Silas, and the magistrates ordered them to be stripped and beaten. After they had been severely flogged, they were thrown into prison, and the jailer was commanded to guard them carefully. Upon receiving such orders, he put them in the inner cell and fastened their feet in the stocks. About midnight Paul and Silas were praying and singing hymns to God, and the other prisoners were listening to them (Acts 16:19-25).

4 When these believers experienced controversy and had disputes among themselves, they turned to prayer.

They had strong leaders who said, "We must make prayer our number one priority."

In those days when the number of disciples was increasing, the Grecian Jews among them complained against the Hebraic Jews because their widows were being overlooked in the daily distribution of food. So the Twelve gathered all the disciples together and said, "It would not be right for us to neglect the ministry of the word of God in order to wait on tables. Brothers, choose seven men from among you who are known to be full of the Spirit and wisdom. We will turn this responsibility over to them and will give our attention to prayer and the ministry of the word" (Acts 6:1-4).

5 When Christians became sick, they called for the elders of the church who prayed over them.

Is any one of you sick? He should call the elders of the church to pray over him and anoint him with oil in the name of the Lord. And the prayer offered in faith will make the sick person well; the Lord will raise him up. If he has sinned, he will be forgiven. Therefore confess your sins to each other and pray for each other so that you may be healed. The prayer of a righteous man is powerful and effective (James 5:14-16).

6 The evangelistic outreach of the early church was rooted in fervent prayer.

When the time was right for the gospel message to be offered to the Gentile world, prayer was at the center of the process that brought Jews and Gentiles together. A Gentile, Cornelius, was seeking to find and know God. As he searched, he "prayed to God regularly" (Acts 10:2). And while this God-fearing Gentile was praying, it was no coincidence that Peter, a Jew, was in prayer when God singled him out to be the historic messenger who would cross racial boundaries and present the gospel to people who had been "without hope and without God in the world" (Ephesians 2:12).

> At Caesarea there was a man named Cornelius, a centurion in what was known as the Italian Regiment. He and all his family were devout and God-fearing; he gave generously to those in need and prayed to God regularly (Acts 10:1, 2).

> About noon the following day as they were on their journey and approaching the city, Peter went up on the roof to pray. He became hungry and wanted something to eat, and while the meal was being prepared, he fell into a trance. He saw heaven opened and something like a large sheet being let down to earth by its four corners. It contained all kinds of four-footed animals, as well as reptiles of the earth and birds of the air. Then a voice told him, "Get up, Peter. Kill and eat." "Surely not, Lord!" Peter replied. "I have never eaten anything impure or unclean." The voice spoke to him a second time, "Do not call anything impure that God has made clean" (Acts 10:9-15).

Furthermore, when the church in Antioch of Syria was preparing to send Christian missionaries throughout the Roman world declaring the message of salvation through Jesus Christ, leaders of that church were fasting and praying. It was the praying of a mission-minded church that undergirded the extensive missionary work of Paul.

> In the church at Antioch there were prophets and teachers: Barnabas, Simeon called Niger, Lucius of Cyrene, Manaen (who had been brought up with Herod the tetrarch) and Saul. While they were worshiping the Lord and fasting, the Holy Spirit said, "Set apart for me Barnabas and Saul for the work to which I have called them." So after they had fasted and prayed, they placed their hands on them and sent them off (Acts 13:1-3).

7 Members of the first-century church enjoyed rich and meaningful fellowship with one another. It was mutual prayer that served as the vital link that kept them connected in the Spirit.

For example, consider examples of the prayer link that existed between Paul and the churches with which he maintained a close working relationship.

I urge you, brothers, by our Lord Jesus Christ and by the love of the Spirit, to join me in my struggle by praying to God for me. Pray that I may be rescued from the unbelievers in Judea and that my service in Jerusalem may be acceptable to the saints there, so that by God's will I may come to you with joy and together with you be refreshed (Romans 15:30-32).

I thank my God every time I remember you. In all my prayers for all of you, I always pray with joy because of your partnership in the gospel from the first day until now, being confident of this, that he who began a good work in you will carry it on to completion until the day of Christ Jesus (Philippians 1:3-6).

And because of this I rejoice. Yes, and I will continue to rejoice, for I know that through your prayers and the help given by the Spirit of Jesus Christ, what has happened to me will turn out for my deliverance. I eagerly expect and hope that I will in no way be ashamed, but will have sufficient courage so that now as always Christ will be exalted in my body, whether by life or by death (Philippians 1:18b-20).

We always thank God, the Father of our Lord Jesus Christ, when we pray for you, because we have heard of your faith in Christ Jesus and of the love you have for all the saints—(Colossians 1:3, 4).

We always thank God for all of you, mentioning you in our prayers. We continually remember before our God and Father your work produced by faith, your labor prompted by love, and your endurance inspired by hope in our Lord Jesus Christ (1 Thessalonians 1:2, 3).

On one occasion when Paul had to say good-bye to Christians from Ephesus—people with whom he had shared a very close and personal relationship—they knelt together and prayed with great emotion.

When he had said this, he knelt down with all of them and prayed. They all wept as they embraced him and kissed him. What grieved them most was his statement that they would never see his face again. Then they accompanied him to the ship (Acts 20:36-38).

8 The early Christians were encouraged to grow and mature in their prayer life.

Paul's words to the churches of Rome, Colossae, and Thessalonica echo the words of instruction and encouragement that he must have given to all churches with whom he worked.

> Be joyful in hope, patient in affliction, and faithful in prayer (Romans 12:12).

> Devote yourselves to prayer, being watchful and thankful (Colossians 4:2).

> Pray continually (1 Thessalonians 5:17).

Devotion to Prayer Made a Difference in the First Century

No doubt about it. These examples make it clear that the early followers of Christ were devoted to prayer. God heard their expressions of praise and cries of petition, and He faithfully responded. The centrality of prayer in the New Testament is clear.

> Then the church throughout Judea, Galilee and Samaria enjoyed a time of peace. It was strengthened; and encouraged by the Holy Spirit, it grew in numbers, living in the fear of the Lord (Acts 9:31).

Devotion to Prayer Keeps the Spirit and Practice of Jesus Alive Within His Church

Jesus was devoted to prayer. In fact, He prayed with great passion.

> During the days of Jesus' life on earth, he offered up prayers and petitions with loud cries and tears to the one who could save him from death, and he was heard because of his reverent submission (Hebrews 5:7).

The greatest illustration of Jesus' intensity in prayer took place in the Garden of Gethsemane prior to His death.

> He withdrew about a stone's throw beyond them, knelt down and prayed, "Father, if You are willing, take this cup from me; yet not my will, but yours be done." And being in anguish, he prayed more earnestly, and his sweat was like drops of blood falling to the ground (Luke 22:41, 42, 44).

In Matthew 6 and Luke 11, we have some of the teaching that Jesus did on prayer. The actual prayer-practice of the Master was so touching and impressive to the disciples that it prompted them to ask Him to teach them how to pray (Luke 11:1). In response to their request, He provided a model of prayer for them to follow. We call it "the Lord's Prayer" even though Jesus did not actually offer these words in prayer to the Father. In this model prayer, Jesus teaches us to approach God as our Father and to pray with a keen sense of trust in and dependency on Him. He teaches us that God is the source of forgiveness and the One to whom glory and honor must always be given.

Our Lord was devoted to prayer. And, even now, as Jesus sits at the right hand of God, He is still praying for us. While we live on earth as resident-aliens, it is wonderful to know that we have a friend and advocate at the right hand of God in heaven who is continually praying for us.

> Who is he that condemns? Christ Jesus, who died—more than that, who was raised to life—is at the right hand of God and is also interceding for us (Romans 8:34).

> Therefore he is able to save completely those who come to God through him, because he always lives to intercede for them (Hebrews 7:25).

Devotion to Prayer Opens the Way for God to Bless

As strangers on this earth, separated from our heavenly homeland, we are never alone if we maintain an open prayer line with God. In fact, this is a communication line that should remain open continually. Verbally or in the spirit, we converse or commune with the Father at all times (1 Thessalonians 5:17). He is always awake and available to hear us—24/7 (Psalm 121:3, 4). No blackouts. No busy signals. No impersonal answering machines. And no dropped calls. Only persistent sin and rebellion on our part can disrupt the link or break the lines. And as we keep an open prayer line with heaven, we discover a powerful source of strength and wisdom during our tough and toilsome journey through this pilgrim land. Take note of some of the specific benefits available to us when we are devoted to prayer.

> **1 When we are devoted to prayer, we discover a dimension of fellowship and friendship with God that is valuable beyond human description.**

Prayer is a way by which we express our faith in a God who is there for us even though we cannot see Him as we see each other. Prayer must begin with an ability to see the "invisible" (Hebrews 11:27). Even though we do not see God visibly or hear God audibly, by faith we know—we know—He's there! He does not cast a shadow. He leaves no footprints in the sand. There are no detectable fingerprints on doorknobs, nor is there a lingering aroma in the room. But He's there!

So how can we relate to a spirit-being if we are not spirit-beings? We are spirit-beings! Could it be that one of our deficiencies in prayer is that we are coming up short when it comes to our ability to perceive the reality of our own spiritual personhood and identity? Think about it. Who is the real you? Who is the "permanent you"? Someone might say, "Here, touch me. See me. You are looking at the real me! Here is my head—my brain. Here is my body—the real me!"

Is that all there is? Is that it? Is that our view and perception of our own reality and personhood? Am I nothing more than an external body that can walk and talk and function biologically? Is there no more to my reality than what can be seen by the human eye or touched with the human hand? If this is all you can see of yourself—a corporeal body and no more—prayer will always be difficult and less than what it can and should be. Could it be that many of us tend to have a tinge of "the Thomas instinct" within us (John 20:24, 29)?

Try this. When you go to your room to pray, how many bodies are there? One. But in that same room, how many spirits are present? Not one, but two! Count them. The spirit of God is there, and the human spirit is there.

> But when you pray, go into your room, close the door and pray to your Father, who is unseen. Then your Father, who sees what is done in secret, will reward you (Matthew 6:6).

This truth is essential to a meaningful prayer life. When we pray, there are two spirit-beings that commune with one another—God and you. So when you pray, don't count bodies. Count spirits! Be keenly aware of the invisible spiritual connection that exists between you and God. Understand that there is a mystery in prayer as your spirit communes with His spirit; a relationship of love, trust, and intimacy is formed.

> From one man he made every nation of men, that they should inhabit the whole earth; and he determined the times set for them and the exact places where they should live. God did this so that men would seek him and perhaps reach out for him and find him, though he is not far from each one of us. For in him we live and move and have our being. As some of your own poets have said, "We are his offspring" (Acts 17:26, 28).

What a tremendous blessing that when we approach the Almighty God in prayer, we are actually talking to our "Abba Father" (Romans 8:15; Galatians 4:6-7). This truth has powerful implications for us. It says a great deal about the manner in which we talk to Him. How does a child talk to his or her daddy—the meaning of "Abba"? This strikes a death blow to artificialness and extreme formalism in prayer. It encourages us to speak in a simple and natural way. Excessive concern over how a prayer may sound to God tends to stifle the natural expression of the heart and block sincerity, earnestness, praise, and confession. We need to cultivate the attitude of the little girl who was praying at her bedside with her dad. Her father coaxed her by saying, "Nancy, speak up. I cannot hear you." She replied, "I'm not talking to you."

2 Devotion to prayer keeps us connected and in touch with our heavenly homeland.

Have you had to leave home and do some traveling in recent days? Sometimes we leave our loved ones and journey to distant places to live among people we do not know. In these situations—especially if they are extended periods of separation—there can be feelings of distress, even homesickness, as we long for the people, the sights, and the sounds of home. Staying connected with those from whom we are separated is so crucial. We may be in touch with these individuals many times in the course of a day. In fact, even before our journey begins, we like to confirm that there are dependable communication links and lines that we can access to stay connected with home. When many miles separate us from home, we feel a strong desire to stay connected with the people we love and depend upon the most. Separation from our loved ones does not lessen our desire to share our joys, sorrows, needs and plans with the folks back home. In fact, our separation only serves to heighten that desire.

Do you see how this same rationale applies to our situation as resident-aliens in this world? Separated from our Father and the homeland of heaven, we treasure and maintain a direct line of communication with our Father through the avenue of prayer. In any relationship, there has to be meaningful communication. Without it, no relationship can thrive. This certainly applies to our relationship with God. How can we really love Him unless we share our heart with Him? How can we begin to think like Him unless we ask Him what He thinks about the situations we face each day? Prayer keeps us connected with the homeland from which we are separated during our temporary pilgrimage on earth.

At my first defense, no one came to my support, but everyone deserted me. May it not be held against them. But the Lord stood at my side and gave me strength, so that through me the message might be fully proclaimed and all the Gentiles might hear it. And I was delivered from the lion's mouth. The Lord will rescue me from every evil attack and will bring me safely to his heavenly kingdom. To him be glory for ever and ever. Amen (2 Timothy 4:16-18).

3 Devotion to prayer strengthens our camarade-rie with fellow believers—those with whom we share heavenly citizenship.

Jesus taught us to pray, "Our Father in heaven...." In using the plural pronoun "our," is there a valuable lesson that when we pray, other persons should be on our hearts, minds, and lips? I must not always approach the Father feeling that I am an only child. To the contrary, I am part of a big family—the church—and have relationships with many spiritual siblings who are just as precious and just as loved by the Father as I am. Like any loving parent, the Father wants us to love each other and treat each other with due respect and kindness. So talking with God in prayer should frequently include other members of God's big family. We should bring their needs before the Father and not just our own.

> For this reason, since the day we heard about you, we have not stopped praying for you and asking God to fill you with the knowledge of his will through all spiritual wisdom and understanding. And we pray this in order that you may live a life worthy of the Lord and may please him in every way: bearing fruit in every good work, growing in the knowledge of God, being strengthened with all power according to his glorious might so that you may have great endurance and patience, and joyfully giving thanks to the Father, who has qualified you to share in the inheritance of the saints in the kingdom of light (Colossians 1:9-12).

This also means praying for the will and strength to forgive those who have sinned against us.

> This, then, is how you should pray:
>
> "Our Father in heaven, hallowed be your name. Your kingdom come, your will be done on earth as it is in heaven. Give us today our daily bread. Forgive us our debts, as we also have forgiven our debtors. And lead us not into temptation, but deliver us from the evil one."
>
> For if you forgive men when they sin against you, your heavenly Father will also forgive you. But if you do not forgive men their sins, your Father will not forgive your sins... (Matthew 6:9-15).

4 Devotion to prayer strengthens our combat with the enemy, Satan.

We are at war! We live on a battlefield—not a playground. We are not serving in a culture that cheers our efforts and rewards our hard work. In this foreign land, we encounter an evil, supernatural, spiritual army that opposes us every step of the way!

> Finally, be strong in the Lord and in his mighty power. Put on the full armor of God so that you can take your stand against the devil's schemes. For our struggle is not against flesh and blood, but against the rulers, against the authorities, against the powers of this dark world and against the spiritual forces of evil in the heavenly realms (Ephesians 6:10-12).

> Those along the path are the ones who hear, and then the devil comes and takes away the word from their hearts, so that they may not believe and be saved (Luke 8:12).

> The god of this age has blinded the minds of unbelievers, so that they cannot see the light of the gospel of the glory of Christ, who is the image of God (2 Corinthians 4:4).

In our efforts to resist the enemy, we must "[p]ut on the full armor of God" and stand firm in the strength of the Lord (Ephesians 6:10-17). Satan will do all that he can to hinder and harm those who serve in the army of God. One of the most powerful resources that we must utilize in the battle with the forces of evil is prayer. In this same context where Paul is describing our spiritual warfare, he writes about the importance of prayer:

> And pray in the Spirit on all occasions with all kinds of prayers and requests. With this in mind, be alert and always keep on praying for all the saints (Ephesians 6:18).

Prayer can be the key factor in deciding whether we are winners or losers in the fight. A full suit of armor coupled with prayer provides all that is necessary for victory. Armor, alone, is not enough. There must be divine power and energy behind the armor. Goliath was strapped with armor, but he lacked the power of God.

> David said to the Philistine, "You come against me with sword and spear and javelin, but I come against you in the name of the LORD Almighty, the God of the armies of Israel, whom you have defied. This day the LORD will hand you over to me, and I'll strike you down and cut off your head. Today I will give the carcasses of the Philistine army to the birds of the air and the beasts of the earth, and the whole world will know that there is a God in Israel. All those gathered here will know that it is not by sword or spear that

the LORD saves; for the battle is the LORD's, and he will give all of you into our hands" (1 Samuel 17:45-47).

This passage is a perfect match with the message of Paul in Ephesians 6. How did Paul begin this entire section that deals with our battle with the forces of evil? "Finally, be strong in the Lord and in his mighty power" (Ephesians 6:10). And, how do we tap His strength and mighty power? "[P]ray in the Spirit" (Ephesians 6:18). Every time we pray, the Holy Spirit participates with us. "[T]he Spirit intercedes for the saints in accordance with God's will" (v. 27). Prayerlessness may be the rankest form of humanism there is—depending on human resources rather than the power of God.

5 Devotion to prayer demonstrates our love and concern for the lost.

Paul's famous missionary journeys were launched with prayer (Acts 13:1-3). In writing to the church in Rome, Paul makes this touching statement which reveals the depth of his love for those who were not saved.

> Brothers, my heart's desire and prayer to God for the Israelites is that they may be saved (Romans 10:1).

Also, to the Christians in Ephesus and Colossae, Paul wrote strong words, which show the powerful connection between prayer and effective evangelism.

> Pray also for me, that whenever I open my mouth, words may be given me so that I will fearlessly make known the mystery of the gospel, for which I am an ambassador in chains. Pray that I may declare it fearlessly, as I should (Ephesians 6:19, 20).

> And pray for us, too, that God may open a door for our message, so that we may proclaim the mystery of Christ, for which I am in chains. Pray that I may proclaim it clearly, as I should. Be wise in the way you act toward outsiders; make the most of every opportunity (Colossians 4:3-5).

6 In response to our willingness to be devoted to prayer, God promises to meet our needs and give us peace in the midst of a troubled world.

When the journey on this earth seems long and the burdens weigh you down, it's prayer that can get you through.

So I say to you: Ask and it will be given to you; seek and you will find; knock and the door will be opened to you. For everyone who asks receives; he who seeks finds; and to him who knocks, the door will be opened. Which of you fathers, if your son asks for a fish, will give him a snake instead? Or if he asks for an egg, will give him a scorpion? If you then, though you are evil, know how to give good gifts to your children, how much more will your Father in heaven give the Holy Spirit to those who ask him! (Luke 11:9-13).

Rejoice in the Lord always. I will say it again: Rejoice! Let your gentleness be evident to all. The Lord is near. Do not be anxious about anything, but in everything, by prayer and petition, with thanksgiving, present your requests to God. And the peace of God, which transcends all understanding, will guard your hearts and your minds in Christ Jesus (Philippians 4:4-7).

What Do We Say When We "Call Home" In Prayer?

As a pilgrim, alien, and stranger on this earth, what thoughts and feelings might be expressed as you speak intimately with your Abba Father in heaven? Here are the words to a prayer that was prayed by this writer on a day when the words of this book were being written.

My God...Father...Abba...Daddy...

I praise and honor Your holy name! Thank you for being such a loving and giving Father. I am richly blessed.

As I make this journey toward home, I just want to stay in touch with You all along the way. Guide my steps and keep me moving forward on the narrow road that leads to life.

I'm not finding this to be an easy trip—it seems like there are always obstacles in my path—things that hurt and hinder. Some days the road is steep. The wind blowing in my face is harsh and cold. It's not easy, Father! This is not surprising since You told me it would be this way.

I'm a mess, Father. I stumble and fall and let You down way too often. And yes, people disappoint and let me down too. Forgive me as I forgive them.

But, You are always there—dependable, faithful, and trustworthy. You have never failed me—never once! Thank You!

At times, I feel so weak—lonely, broken, and afraid. Give me strength to persevere when I get tired. Give me tenacity to endure when I feel overwhelmed. Help me never to quit!

Father, I ask for more patience and love as I deal with difficult relationships—even people that I love dearly. Help me to love them as You have loved me.

Extend Your favor as I struggle to carry out the mission You have given me during my brief residency on earth. I want to live with the heart of a servant, but my tendency to be selfish makes it tough. So, discipline me, Father. You and I both know I need it.

Help me to encourage my fellow pilgrims. Help me to be a light to folks around me who are trapped in darkness. Keep me sensitive to the needs of others.

And Daddy, enable me to be faithful to the end of the way.

Leave the light on for me, Father, as I continue to move in Your direction. And at last, when I leave this foreign country and arrive home, I look forward to walking through that unlocked door and experiencing a warm Fatherly embrace—all because of Your love and patience!

I get excited when I think about sitting at Your table in the homeland—finding my own name written in red with the blood of my Jesus. Your grace is so amazing!

And, there in Your presence—in that new heaven and new earth, may I experience a level of peace and joy that I have never known as I worship and serve You forever and forever!

Father, with the help of Your Spirit, I'll be home soon.

Through Jesus I pray!
Amen!

Practicing the Christian Disciplines Is a Choice

Being devoted "to the apostles' teaching and to the fellowship, to the breaking of bread and to prayer" (Acts 2:42) cannot begin or be sustained unless we are willing to cooperate with God and exercise personal discipline. We must make the choice and exercise the discipline.

While the practice of spiritual disciplines can never be relied upon as the basis for our salvation—only the atoning work of Jesus can do this—these and other such disciplines are crucial and necessary to our sanctification. Spiritual disciplines open the door for Jesus to live powerfully within us. He knocks at the door to your heart. He wants to enter. But, He will not kick down the door and force His way inside (Revelation 3:14-20). Will you open the door to your heart by devoting yourself to the apostles' teaching, the fellowship, the breaking of bread, and prayer? The choice is yours.

FOR FURTHER DISCUSSION AND INTERACTION

1 Of the four spiritual disciplines that we have studied—devotion to the apostles' doctrine, the fellowship, the breaking of bread, and prayer—which ones are easiest for you to practice? Which are the most difficult? Explain your responses.

2 As you look back on your early spiritual formation and training—in the home and in the church—share your feelings about the emphasis that was given to prayer. What was strong about your early training? What was weak and inadequate? What are you doing or planning to do to teach your children the significance of prayer?

3 As you consider today's culture and the daily environment in which you function, what conditions and factors dull and deaden a strong view of and emphasis on prayer? Are there influences in your life which continually strengthen and encourage the practice of prayer?

4 What ideas do you have for enhancing the image of the church as a house of prayer?

5 What thoughts or feelings come to your mind as you envision yourself as a living stone in the temple of God (1 Peter 2:4-10)?

6 As you ponder the vital role that prayer played in the lives of the first-century Christians, what comes to your mind as you consider the role that prayer plays in the church where you are a member? If you feel that there are significant differences, can you offer ideas as to why these differences exist?

7 Offer three practical suggestions as to how Christians in the twenty-first century can improve their efforts to be devoted to prayer.

8 To the extent that you are willing, share with others the specific steps that you have taken to improve the quality of your personal prayer life.

9 Do you agree or disagree with the statement that appears in this chapter, "Prayer must begin with an ability to see the invisible" (Hebrews 11:27)? How do you think a statement like this affects the thinking of the majority of people with whom we rub shoulders daily?

10 Based on the material in this chapter that is related to the work of evangelism, why are many people still unsaved and living in the darkness of sin (2 Corinthians 4:4)?

11 Can you cite an example in your life where God answered prayer? Can you refer to a time when, in the midst of difficulty, God provided a peace that surpassed human understanding?

CITIZENS OF HEAVEN—RESIDENTS OF EARTH

Be Diligent—Citizenship Calls for Mission to the World (Part 1)

The Missionary God and His Missionary People

As citizens of heaven residing on earth, we are strangers in a foreign land. While we are here, God has commissioned us to deliver the message of His love and grace to our fellow residents of earth. If we are living in a foreign land and we have a mission to the people around us, what does that make us? Missionaries for God!

To be passionate about our mission, we must understand something about the heart of our God. In His very nature, He is a missionary God. Before the world was created, He saw the terrible mess that humans would make with the freedom He would give them, and planned for a very costly rescue and clean-up operation.

> For you know that it was not with perishable things such as silver or gold that you were redeemed from the empty way of life handed down to you from your forefathers, but with the precious blood of Christ, a lamb without blemish or defect. He was chosen before the creation of the world, but was revealed in these last times for your sake (1 Peter 1:18-20).

> For he chose us in him before the creation of the world to be holy and blameless in his sight (Ephesians 1:4).

> Who has saved us and called us to a holy life—not because of anything we have done but because of his own purpose and grace. This grace was given us in Christ Jesus before the beginning of time (2 Timothy 1:9).

> [Jesus], the Lamb that was slain from the creation of the world (Revelation 13:8).

It happened just as God had envisioned. In the Garden of Eden, Adam and Eve rejected God's leadership and disobeyed His clear commands. Then, in shame, they ran away and attempted to hide from the One whose heart they had broken. But, their hiding was futile. Brokenhearted fathers don't give up easily on stubborn children. God continued His search. Can you hear the voice of this concerned and caring Father as He walked up and down the pathways of Eden calling out to His rebellious children, "Where are you?" (Genesis 3: 9). This is our missionary God.

Centuries later, this same loving Father is still calling out to His wayward kids, "Where are you? Won't you come home to Me?" And how does He send that call today? How does He express His love and concern for children who have strayed and lost their way? It's amazing! Today, the appealing call of this missionary God goes out through the lives of His missionary people—the citizens of heaven. Our efforts to reach out to lost people is just an extension of what God has been doing since the very beginning—loving, seeking, rescuing, and saving sinners. We are the pipelines through which God wants to channel the water of life into the lives of people who are dying of spiritual thirst. Because of our heavenly citizenship, we do have an earthly calling. We are the missionary people of the missionary God.

> All this is from God, who reconciled us to himself through Christ and gave us the ministry of reconciliation: that God was reconciling the world to himself in Christ, not counting men's sins against them. And he has committed to us the message of reconciliation. We are therefore Christ's ambassadors, as though God were making his appeal through us. We implore you on Christ's behalf: Be reconciled to God (2 Corinthians 5:18-20).

Jesus Loved Lost People—and So Must We

Jesus left heaven to become personally involved in the great rescue mission of sinners on earth. He had a burning love for lost people (Luke 4:14-21). His passion was so great that members of His own family concluded, "He is out of his mind" (Mark 3:20, 21).

> For the Son of Man came to seek and to save what was lost (Luke 19:10).

> For even the Son of Man did not come to be served, but to serve, and to give his life as a ransom for many (Mark 10:45).

Jesus wants the same burning love to show in the lives of His followers. We see it in the disciples of the first century. In fact, they were so passionate about their Messiah, their mission, and their message that they were, at times, viewed by some as being drunk (Acts 2:15), unschooled (4:13), illegal (5:28), disorderly (17:6), foolish (1 Corinthians 4:10), and insane (Acts 26:24).

But, is such love for lost people clearly showing in the lives of Christians today? As one questioner painfully put it, "Have we, in our day, turned the sword of the Spirit—the Word of God—into a back scratcher?"

How do we get the missionary movement moving once again? How do we refocus on the crucial mission before us and rekindle our love for lost people? How do we motivate citizens of heaven to be missionaries on earth?

Jesus Has a Plan to Reach Lost People— We Are a Vital Part of the Plan

When Jesus was on earth, He announced a plan by which all of His followers would participate in the work of rescuing lost people. This plan called for citizens of heaven to reside in the world, but not be of the world (John 17:14-18). In too many cases, this plan has been reversed. Too many citizens of heaven are of the world but not in it. That is, they are not in the dark and decaying world as active and aggressive agents of light and life for Jesus Christ.

To His disciples, Jesus' instructions are clear—not easy, but clear. He says

> You are the salt of the earth. But if the salt loses its saltiness, how can it be made salty again? It is no longer good for anything, except to be thrown out and trampled by men (Matthew 5:13).

> You are the light of the world. A city on a hill cannot be hidden. Neither do people light a lamp and put it under a bowl. Instead they put it on its stand, and it gives light to everyone in the house. In the same way, let your light shine before men, that they may see your good deeds and praise your Father in heaven (Matthew 5:14-16).

When Jesus walked on the earth, salt and light were common in every home. Salt was an essential item—not just to season food, but more importantly, to preserve it. With no refrigeration, fresh meat would quickly go bad. Thus, salt was rubbed into meat to retard spoilage and keep it from rotting. Light was also an essential item. With no electricity, an oil lamp would be placed on a stand in the room so that light could penetrate the darkness and make it possible for all to see.

This plan for us to be salt and light is a powerful concept. Jesus lifts us out of the decay and the darkness of this godless world. He cleanses us and infuses His life and light—made possible by His death and resurrection (Ephesians 2:1-5). He fills us with His Spirit and teaches us to live with His heart and think with His mind (4:17-24). Then, He sends us back into the very environment from which He called us and instructs us to be salt in the earth and light in the world (2:8-10). With the culture of heaven influencing our lives, we are to be fully devoted to the daily task of sharing this life-giving culture in a world that we no longer view as our home. This makes us missionaries for Christ.

Don't Lose Your Saltiness! Don't Let Your Light Dim—or Go Out

An English bishop once said, "Everywhere first-century Christians went, there was a revolution. Everywhere I go they serve tea." Why would one generation of disciples trigger a revolution while the other does little more than prompt the serving of tea? Could it be that those early believers had a better grasp on the powerful implications of what it means to be salt, bringing the culture of heaven into the culture of earth? Could it be that they saw themselves as spiritual commandos whose primary purpose was to penetrate the unconquered, non-Christian territory of this world and shine for Christ in places where His light had never penetrated?

These salty people stirred things up because they crossed into enemy space and challenged the evil powers of this dark world with the light of the gospel of heaven. With boldness, these people went public with their heavenly citizenship, and the world hated them because of it. These early disciples took seriously the mandate that Jesus gave His followers before He left this world.

Then Jesus came to them and said, "All authority in heaven and on earth has been given to me. Therefore go and make disciples of all nations, baptizing them in the name of the Father and of the Son and of the Holy Spirit, and teaching them to obey everything I have commanded you. And surely I am with you always, to the very end of the age" (Matthew 28:18-20).

He said to them, "Go into all the world and preach the good news to all creation. Whoever believes and is baptized will be saved, but whoever does not believe will be condemned" (Mark 16:15, 16).

Then someone came and said, "Look! The men you put in jail are standing in the temple courts teaching the people." At that, the captain went with his officers and brought the apostles. They did not use force, because they feared that the people would stone them. Having brought the apostles, they made them appear before the Sanhedrin to be questioned by the high priest. "We gave you strict orders not to teach in this name," he said. "Yet you have filled Jerusalem with your teaching..." (Acts 5:25-28).

And Saul was there, giving approval to his death. On that day a great persecution broke out against the church at Jerusalem, and all except the apostles were scattered throughout Judea and Samaria. Godly men buried Stephen and mourned deeply for him. But Saul began to destroy the church. Going from house to house, he dragged off men and women and put them in prison. Those who had been scattered preached the word wherever they went (Acts 8:1-4).

But the Jews were jealous; so they rounded up some bad characters from the marketplace, formed a mob and started a riot in the city. They rushed to Jason's house in search of Paul and Silas in order to bring them out to the crowd. But when they did not find them, they dragged Jason and some other brothers before the city officials, shouting: "These men who have caused trouble all over the world have now come here..." (Acts 17:5, 6).

For I have a great sense of obligation to people in both the civilized world and the rest of the world, to the educated and uneducated alike. So I am eager to come to you in Rome, too, to preach the Good News. For I am not ashamed of this Good News about Christ. It is the power of God at work, saving everyone who believes—the Jew first and also the Gentile (Romans 1:14-16 NLT).

But now he has reconciled you by Christ's physical body through death to present you holy in his sight, without blemish and free from accusation—if you continue in your faith, established and firm, not moved from the hope held out in the gospel. This is the gospel that you heard and that has been proclaimed to every creature under heaven, and of which I, Paul, have become a servant (Colossians 1:22, 23).

Leave Your Bunker—Move Out into the Lost World

As missionaries for Jesus Christ, we must think "evangelism" every day in all we do. Reaching lost people with the saving message of Jesus is to be our life-style—not just something we do occasionally. We deliver the message to our fellow residents with great love and tenderness, yet we pursue the task with great courage and boldness. Our daily manner of life—the way we think, act, and speak—is to send the message that we have "been with Jesus." As people observe our lives, the marks and signs of heavenly citizenship must show through (Acts 4:13). The testimony of our lives before the world is crucial if people are to believe the message of our lips.

This means that we must find creative ways to infiltrate the world and have contact with lost people. Christians who go to an extreme to avoid being of the world run the risk of becoming so disengaged that their potential salti-ness is neutralized. As wonderful and refreshing as Christian associations may be, the fact remains that we must not dig our foxholes of fellowship so deep that we become like soldiers who lose contact with the enemy. Weapons of warfare that are clean, loaded, and powerful are of no value if they are stored away miles from the battle zone.

Of course, there is a sense in which citizens of heaven are to be separat-ed from the world (2 Corinthians 6:14-7:1; James 4:4). We must never get ourselves entangled in false beliefs or sinful behaviors that would defile us or distract others. However, in order to carry out our responsibilities to the people of this world, we must be ready and willing to enter the turbulent waters of our culture and carry the lifeline of the gospel of hope to those who are sinking. As citizens of heaven, we must be good neighbors to our fellow residents of earth who are hopelessly trying to figure out the meaning and purpose of a few years of citizenship in this world.

We Must Be Students of the Word—and the Lost World

Someone has correctly said that the church always faces the twin dangers of cultural captivity and cultural irrelevance. True, we must know God's revelation—His Word. But we must also know something about the world we are trying to reach. This fact is confirmed when you study the life and work of Paul. He knew the Word. But, he also knew the world around him. While never compromising the gospel, he presented his message with a keen awareness of his immediate surroundings.

> Though I am free and belong to no man, I make myself a slave to everyone, to win as many as possible. To the Jews I became like a Jew, to win the Jews. To those under the law I became like one under the law (though I myself am not under the law), so as to win those under the law. To those not having the law, I became like one not having the law (though I am not free from God's law but am under Christ's law), so as to win those not having the law. To the weak I became weak, to win the weak. I have become all things to all men so that by all possible means I might save some. I do all this for the sake of the gospel, that I may share in its blessings (1 Corinthians 9:19-23).

Paul's method and manner were in perfect alignment with the teaching of Jesus. The Lord carefully prepared His men for their difficult mission on the earth. Because they were going to be salt—not sugar—in the world, Jesus helped them to understand the hostility that they would encounter. He said

> I am sending you out like sheep among wolves. Therefore be as shrewd as snakes and as innocent as doves (Matthew 10:16).

There was no effort to hide the danger of the mission. Jesus told His men that the world would be wolfish—hostile. Yet He did not want them to be sheepish—helpless and defenseless. He did urge them to be dovelike—gentle and harmless. And He also called for them to be serpentlike—wise, alert, and aware. These were the requirements if they were to be effective and efficient missionaries for Him.

In the same way, we must be adequately prepared for our mission in today's world. This requires that we know something about the people we are trying to reach and the culture we are seeking to change for God.

Evil Forces Affecting the People We Are to Reach

In Chapter 4, an effort was made to explain some of the major philosophical influences that are fueling many of the unhealthy and unholy trends in today's society. The goal was to identify the basic tenants and core beliefs of secularism, humanism, relativism, pluralism, narcissism, and hedonism. In the remainder of this chapter, we will build on that foundation by attempting to understand how the moral and spiritual poisons that flow within those philosophical roots are now showing up as toxic fruits in the daily beliefs and behaviors of many people around us.

How long has it been since you spoke about a controversial, cultural, or religious topic with a stranger at Starbucks, an associate at work, or a neighbor on your street? For example, how long has it been since you openly shared your conviction that fellowship with God is experienced only through Jesus Christ—not the religion of one's choice (John 14:6; Acts 4:12)? When was the last time you openly admitted that you believe God's beautiful plan for marriage calls for a monogamous relationship between one man and one woman? How long has it been since you lovingly and courageously let it be known that you embrace the biblical view that "[t]here is one body...one Spirit...one hope...one Lord, one faith, one baptism [and only] one God" (Ephesians 4:4-6)? How long has it been? And, if confronted with such views and values, how would you expect a stranger at Starbucks, an associate at work, or a neighbor on the block to respond?

Clearly, there are numerous issues that can quickly turn volatile when the tight laws of heaven meet head-on with the loose ways of earth. Culture war can break out when the ways of God confront and contradict the ways of man. Prepare for strong resistance if you dare to go public with your heavenly influenced convictions. If you dare to speak up, you are likely to discover that seismic changes have occurred in the American culture. Common assumptions that were once made about most of our fellow citizens can no longer be made. The religious, moral, and political landscapes have changed drastically, and continue to change by the hour. As Yogi Berra has said, "The future ain't what it used to be."

Our Mission into Territory That Is Not Jesus-Friendly

How do we accurately describe this world into which we must go as missionaries for Christ? Several familiar labels are being used to characterize the mindset of today's new way of thinking. Some have decided that we are living in a post-Christian era. Others are more optimistic and call it a pre-Christian period. And still others have labeled it as the postmodern age.

However you may choose to label the prevailing spirit of our age, the harsh reality is that we are watching biblical doctrines being denied, moral boundaries being moved, and social standards being lowered. What we are witnessing is not merely post-Judeo-Christian activity, but anti-Judeo-Christian hostility. And who are the strongest proponents and promoters of this new way of thinking and living? They are powerful people in the arts and entertainment industry, influencial people in the field of mass media with all of its powerful outlets, and scholarly individuals in modern universities across the land. Even some of our national leaders who sit in seats of power feel no sense of responsibility or accountability to the God of the Bible. This being true, it can only mean that these troublesome trends are likely to continue indefinitely. It also indicates that these ideas will have a significant impact on many of our young people for years to come. So be prepared! As missionaries of Christ, we are entering hostile territory that may not be Jesus-friendly.

The Fruits of Secularistic Humanism We Are Likely to Encounter

The poisonous roots of Secularistic Humanism and all that accompanies it lead to toxic fruits that appear in people's lives. Listed below are description of ten false assumptions that are adversely and dangerously affecting the people of our culture. These conditions have a direct impact on our efforts to reach them with the gospel. In fact, some of these cultural waves have washed upon the doorsteps of many modern-day religious organizations. How deep is the water where you are? Thankfully, there are places and pockets in our society where these ideas do not rule the day. However, the trends and tendencies are spreading rapidly.

Pause and take a deep breath of heavenly oxygen because you are about to wade through some of the polluted conditions that exist in an earthly culture that is living in rebellion to God. Evaluate each of these false beliefs in light of what you are witnessing in your daily world as a missionary of Christ.

> **False Assumption 1: Humans come to know God through their own subjective experiences.**

Since there is no reliable and objective resource such as the Bible to guide this process, each person must see and relate to God based on the people, the places, and the perceptions within his or her own life. In today's restaurants, we build our own sandwiches. In today's religious culture, we build our own gods. By carefully observing what is seen externally and remaining sensitive to what is felt internally, each individual can come to know and relate to his or her own designer god. The fact that this approach frequently leads to very different and contradictory ideas about God is not a problem because there is no universal and objective truth to define God's nature for us. In the end, we have multiple gods—each shaped by an individual's subjective experiences, thoughts, and feelings.

False Assumption 2: There is no objective truth about which we can be certain and on which we can build our lives.

The Bible cannot be viewed as a reliable guide for everyone. There is no universal truth that is to be discovered—personalized truth is to be created. Whatever you think is true is true for you. Advocates say, "Don't impose your beliefs and values on me. Allow me to decide what I am willing to embrace as true and false within my frame of reference." This view of and approach to truth explains why Christianity is under attack. Since the Bible claims to be the universal truth for everyone and declares that all other religions are false, many are incensed. To believe that Jesus is "the way, the truth, and the life"(John 14:6) for all people is viewed as intolerance and bigotry of the worst kind. Christians have their truth. Muslims have their truth. Scientology has its truth. You have your truth. And as I discover what works for me, I have my truth.

False Assumption 3: The exclusive claim of Jesus to be Immanuel—God with us—cannot be believed.

Even the idea that man needs a savior is viewed as a manipulative action designed to put power in the hands of those who proclaim Jesus as the way of salvation. Such narrow- minded teachers are labeled as "power mongers" who are out to demean and destroy all other "religions," "lords," and "saviors." Many today argue that we must be willing and eager to accept everything that is attractive and good from all religions, all saviors, and all lords.

False Assumption 4: Language and words cannot be dependable instruments for communicating objective and universal truth for all people.

Language—words—are slick and slippery, which means it is impossible to settle on meanings. Because all words can have very different meanings for each hearer, it is impossible to accurately communicate uniform teaching that can be understood and defended in any community. In fact, truth and morals are discovered within the context of a particular community, and they vary from one community to another. This explains why many in today's culture prefer dialogue to doctrine, conversation over preaching, and questions instead of answers. People who know, and know that they know, are viewed with suspicion—or hatred. There is always an alternate reading. Listeners are continually looking for the "but" in every statement of fact. Humility is viewed as having questions, qualms, and queries regarding anything that sounds sure and certain. It is considered unspiritual and haughty to speak with authority regarding any biblical truth. If words cannot hold their meanings, then even the Bible cannot have unchanging meaning. Thus, we dare not take firm positions on anything—all the way from sex to salvation.

False Assumption 5: Sin is an unhelpful, undesirable, and socially unacceptable word in today's culture.

For a growing number of people, sin is no longer a moral and spiritual failure due to disobedience of God's revealed will in the Scriptures. Instead, it is viewed as a social or behavioral problem. Damage is done when humans are made to feel guilty simply because they act on their natural desires and needs. You dare not call an action a sin if it is legal, consensual, and helpful to someone personally. Perhaps the most often quoted Bible verse in today's morally confused society is, "Judge not, that you be not judged" (Matthew 7:1 NKJV). The concept of sin has been replaced with shame. Sin implies that I have violated the standards of God. Shame has more to do with the idea that I may have offended human standards. The solution to spiritual guilt and the solution to societal shame are two very different things—the former demands a Savior, while the latter calls for some suitable solution.

False Assumption 6: The doctrine of hell is the ultimate and unacceptable intolerance.

Because there is no sin, there can be no hell. The idea that an offended God would punish people in such a place of torment is considered, by many, the ultimate transgression. Because there is no sin and no hell, why should we live with a fear of God?

False Assumption 7: The noblest mission for humans is to make this world a better place.

If there are rewards to be received at the end of life in this world, they will be given to those who are involved in noble humanitarian efforts. Because people are not viewed as sinners in need of a Savior, the highest human calling becomes the work of improving social conditions and soothing emotional pain on this earth. Evangelism is replaced by social good deeds as the primary mission of the church. The ultimate goal is to make this world a better place. The secularists in today's world are not able to see that the gospel does more than solve the problems we have—it solves the problem that we are.

False Assumption 8: The primary goal of church assemblies is to create an emotional experience for attendees.

The new mindset in today's narcissistic culture has also affected the nature of our church assemblies. In many religious gatherings on Sunday morning, it is more important to stimulate the emotions than it is to teach the Word of God. The main goal in preaching is to create an experience rather than to present the demands of objective truth from the Bible. Thus, doctrinal substance has been exchanged for entertainment and sensory stimulation. Rather than the Bible being taught as the authoritative Word of God, it is presented in a shallow manner as a collection of interesting stories. Such a mindset leads to an overall dumbing-down process that continues to affect the church-at-large.

False Assumption 9: The world has changed the way it views and accepts truth. Therefore the church must change the way it approaches the world—we must be relevant at all costs.

With savvy marketing schemes, we must be seeker sensitive by avoiding objectionable and irritating topics such as blood atonement, salvation through Jesus only, the authority of the Bible, the sinfulness of homosexuality and abortion, a day of judgment, or the existence of heaven and hell. Beliefs, standards, and methods must accommodate the modern culture through a nonoffensive approach to evangelism. If the world considers a particular message outdated and unpopular, it must be altered so that the modern seeker experiences minimal discomfort. God-based and Bible-based spirituality is out, and consumer-based spirituality is in. Rather than the bold teaching and preaching of biblical truth, we should move toward conversations that require nothing.

One religious leader said, "As members of the army of God, we must not see ourselves as one religious army at war with all other religious armies, but as one of many religious armies fighting for the god of choice against evil, falsehood, destruction, darkness, and injustice. We must be about the universal march for peace in the world and reject anything and everything that could be interpreted by the modern world as insensitive, unloving, exclusive, or judgmental." Almost everybody is going to heaven—if there is one!

Our Mission in the Midst of the Mess—What Can We Do?

As missionaries for Christ, how are we to view our mission in the midst of such biblical illiteracy and cultural decline? Can we ignore these conditions and hope they go away? No! Can we make a big wish and expect tomorrow to be like yesterday? No!

As undesirable as these cultural conditions may be, they fairly represent the society in which we are to function as salt and light. These guidelines impact the way public discourse is carried on, civil law is enacted, cultural entertainment is designed, public opinion is shaped, and sadly, religious causes are designed. For many citizens of heaven across the land, these views are painfully descriptive of the people with whom we rub shoulders daily—the residents of earth we are called to love and evangelize.

Today, we need children of Issachar. Living in a time when the monarchies of Saul and David were in chaos and the people were anxious about the future, there were the sons of Issachar who "understood the times and knew what Israel should do" (I Chronicles 12:32). Where are the sons of Issachar today? How we need them!

What are we to do? We can love lost people even if we are not loved in return. We can continue to value and defend the truth of the gospel even when its power is not understood or appreciated. We can be bold for Christ even when our boldness may be falsely labeled as insensitivity. We can be faithful to our God even when we are not popular with our peers. As strangers and aliens in this strange world, we can be faithful to our calling as missionaries for Christ.

Paul and Timothy were partners in evangelism in the first century—in a culture very similar to ours. The words that Paul wrote to his missionary coworker, Timothy, speak loud and clear to us—the missionary people of God in the twenty-first century!

In the presence of God and of Christ Jesus, who will judge the living and the dead, and in view of his appearing and his kingdom, I give you this charge: Preach the Word; be prepared in season and out of season; correct, rebuke and encourage—with great patience and careful instruction. For the time will come when men will not put up with sound doctrine. Instead, to suit their own desires, they will gather around them a great number of teachers to say what their itching ears want to hear. They will turn their ears away from the truth and turn aside to myths. But you, keep your head in all situations, endure hardship, do the work of an evangelist, discharge all the duties of your ministry. For I am already being poured out like a drink offering, and the time has come for my departure. I have fought the good fight, I have finished the race, I have kept the faith. Now there is in store for me the crown of righteousness, which the Lord, the righteous Judge, will award to me on that day—and not only to me, but also to all who have longed for his appearing (2 Timothy 4:1-8).

FOR FURTHER DISCUSSION AND INTERACTION

1   As you see it, is it fair and reasonable to expect disciples in the twenty-first century to have the same love for lost people that characterized the missionaries of Christ in the first century? Explain.

2   Give three reasons why it is difficult to be in the world without being of the world. What is it about the world that can be so appealing and alluring to modern-day believers?

3   On a scale of 1-10 (with 10 being the best and highest score), how would you rate yourself when it comes to being salt to the earth and light to the world? How would you rate the local church where you worship? Are you seeing revolutions or the serving of tea?

4   Would you be willing to share with a fellow citizen of heaven some particular struggle that represents a clash in your life between the cultures of heaven and earth? Where are you hurting and feeling weak? Perhaps this conversation should occur in private with a trusted brother or sister. Or, if you are willing, your transparency could motivate others around you to be confessional and ask for support.

5   Using these passages—Acts 21:17-26, Galatians 2:11-14, and Acts 17:16-34—discuss the idea that Paul carried on his evangelistic work with a keen awareness of the cultural context in which he was working.

6   Do you think conditions in the first century made it harder or easier for believers to evangelize than for us in the twenty-first century?

7   Which is the greater danger for most Christians today: (1) remaining too detached from the world and thus being ineffective as salt and light, or, (2) being too much like the world and thus neutralizing the potency of our Christian testimony? Discuss the twin dangers of cultural captivity and cultural irrelevance.

8   What is the practical difference between viewing evangelism as a lifestyle and viewing it as a particular program of the church?

9   Identify practical ways by which believers today can be salt and light in the political arena, the local community, and the workplace. Identify a person within your fellowship who has been creative and effective in this area and ask this individual to share with your group.

10 Evaluate and access the level of hostility that exists in your community toward Christian beliefs and values.

11 Identify specific beliefs and behaviors within your daily environment (home, school, workplace, community, etc.) which clearly reflect a "new" way of thinking, deciding, and living on the part of your peers.

12 Read 2 Timothy 4:1-8. Which part of this passage is especially meaningful to you as you think about the challenges we face in our efforts to evangelize effectively and efficiently? As you see it, which portion of this passage addresses a particular hindrance to evangelism in today's church?

CITIZENS OF HEAVEN—RESIDENTS OF EARTH

Be Diligent—Citizenship Calls for Mission to the World (Part 2)

Our Huge Mission and God's Big Promise

As citizens of heaven residing on earth, we've been given a big command, which entails a huge assignment. The commander is Jesus, and the assignment we have been given is as follows:

> All authority in heaven and on earth has been given to me. Therefore go and make disciples of all nations, baptizing them in the name of the Father and of the Son and of the Holy Spirit, and teaching them to obey everything I have commanded you (Matthew 28:18b, 20a).

Make disciples of all nations. What a gigantic task! But don't stop reading—there is more to what Jesus said. Not only did He give us a big command—along with it He made a big promise. Jesus went on to say

> And surely I am with you always, to the very end of the age (Matthew 28:20b).

Jesus said, "Go. And as you go, I will go with you." By relying on His big promise, we can discover everything that we need to undertake and obey His big command. And don't forget those encouraging words Jesus spoke to that band of ordinary men in the first century that accepted the call of discipleship and became the first missionaries of Christ.

> As Jesus walked beside the Sea of Galilee, he saw Simon and his brother Andrew casting a net into the lake, for they were fishermen. "Come, follow me," Jesus said, "and I will make you fishers of men." At once they left their nets and followed him (Mark 1:16-18).

Jesus told these fishers of fish to become fishers of men. In the same breath, He was assuring them that He would equip them for the task. So in the two passages cited above, we have Jesus—our missionary Lord—promising to be with us as we go out to make disciples and assuring us that He will equip us as we launch out to fish for men. Big challenges. But also big promises. This great fishing expedition that started more than two thousand years ago is still going on today. Jesus, the Great Fisherman, is willing to be right there in the boat with us.

Fishing for Fish—and Fishing for Men

It's always exciting to catch fish. But in order for this to happen, certain conditions have to be met. First, if a person wants to catch fish, he must go where the fish are. At some point, he must lay aside the training manuals on how to be a good fisherman and go to the water where the fish live. Once there, a person must put a baited hook in the water, which means equipment must be obtained. You don't just tie a hook on the end of a string and expect to catch a fish. Also, it is understood that a good fisherman needs to be knowledgeable about other factors that may affect his catch—weather conditions, fish habitats, and effective techniques. Even a person's mental attitude will have an impact on his success or failure. A good fisherman has to be patient—perseverance is a must on those days when the fish are not biting.

Similarly, if we are to be successful in fishing for men, there are pertinent facts and factors that must be taken into account. There is important information we need to know. There are conditions we need to understand. There are skills we need to perfect. And, there are attitudes and feelings we need to have. This mission to fish for men and make disciples would be overwhelming were it not for those reassuring promises to help us from Jesus. Let's highlight them one more time. As we enter the hostile world to make disciples, what does Jesus promise? He says, "I will be with you." And as we prepare to fish for men, what does Jesus say He will do? He says, "Follow me and I will make you fishers of men." Our responsibility is to undertake the big mission with full assurance that Jesus will keep His big promises by being with us and enabling us for the task at hand.

In this chapter, our goal will be to highlight some of the facts and conditions related to our work as missionaries for Christ. We will identify some of the feelings we need to have and some of the attitudes we need to display. Using Jesus as our model and the Scriptures as our guide, we will allow the Master Fisherman to instruct us on how to be good fishers for men.

1 To Be Effective as Missionaries for Christ, We Must Understand the Dangerous Condition of Lost People.

Jesus Saw the Hopeless Condition of Sinners— and He Cared

As Jesus looked into the faces of lost people, He understood the horrible reality of their spiritual condition. He saw that they were blinded to God and enslaved to sin—and He deeply cared. In fact, His concern for sinners was so intense that He wept over their condition. His cheeks were wet with tears of love and concern. Too often, our cheeks are dry because of apathy and ignorance. What did Jesus know and understand about lost people that we may be missing?

With keen spiritual eyesight and insight, Jesus could see beyond the external façade of an individual. For example, when an unsaved wealthy man approached Jesus, the external trinkets of gold and silver did not distract Him—He just saw a spiritual beggar whose life was completely empty of the things that really matter. When a highly-educated lost person came into the presence of Jesus, He was never awed by the impressive list of titles and degrees behind the person's name—He just saw the sad condition of a person who was spiritually illiterate. When Jesus witnessed an unbeliever who appeared to be the life of the party on earth, He grieved because He saw a person whose name was missing from the list of those who would be invited to celebrate at God's banquet table in heaven.

Jesus' ability to see spiritual reality in the lives of lost people was never blocked by external conditions or physical appearances. He understood that what you saw on the outside of a person was not necessarily what existed on the inside. In fact, He knew that external signs of power and life frequently served as a cover-up for internal weakness and death. Jesus not only saw to people, He saw *through* them. Most important of all, Jesus was deeply touched when He encountered people whose lives were plagued by the deadly cancer of sin.

Do We See the Dangerous Condition of Lost People— and Do We Care?

As citizens of heaven who have an important mission on this earth, we must see—really see—the dangerous and desperate condition of lost people. And we must deeply care. How do the Scriptures describe the serious plight of our fellow residents on earth to whom we are sent as missionaries?

> As for you, you were dead in your transgressions and sins, in which you used to live when you followed the ways of this world and of the ruler of the kingdom of the air, the spirit who is now at work in those who are disobedient. All of us also lived among them at one time, gratifying the cravings of our sinful nature and following its desires and thoughts. Like the rest, we were by nature objects of wrath (Ephesians 2:1-3).

[R]emember that at that time you were separate from Christ, excluded from citizenship in Israel and foreigners to the covenants of the promise, without hope and without God in the world (Ephesians 2:12).

The lost people of this world are in serious trouble. How are you responding as a missionary for Christ? Do you suppose your rescue efforts would be different if you could see—literally see—the horrible spiritual condition of lost people around you? Imagine the horror of being able to smell the stench of their spiritual deadness. Or what if you could see the literal chains that Satan is using to keep them in spiritual bondage? Suppose when you looked at your loved ones and neighbors who are lost you could literally see the blindfolds being used by the enemy to keep them in spiritual darkness—blinded to the power of the gospel. If the spiritual captivity of people in this world was made literal and visible in these ways, how concerned would you be and how urgently might you act to do something about their dilemma?

> The god of this age has blinded the minds of unbelievers, so that they cannot see the light of the gospel of the glory of Christ, who is the image of God (2 Corinthians 4:4).

> The sinful mind is hostile to God. It does not submit to God's law, nor can it do so. Those controlled by the sinful nature cannot please God (Romans 8:7, 8).

The sad reality is that the lost people of this world really are spiritually blinded, bound, and dead. This is reality. They are under the power of the evil one—Satan. They do not perceive the danger they are in. They cannot see their one way of escape. Their problem is more than a mere lack of information. Their peril is created by much more than the fact that they may be stubborn or stupid. The real problem goes much deeper. The lost people with whom we rub shoulders every day—people who may appear to be so free and so fabulous—are actually living under the power of Satan and enslaved by their own sinful passions and pleasures.

> At one time we too were foolish, disobedient, deceived and enslaved by all kinds of passions and pleasures. We lived in malice and envy, being hated and hating one another (Titus 3:3).

> They are darkened in their understanding and separated from the life of God because of the ignorance that is in them due to the hardening of their hearts (Ephesians 4:18).

If unsaved people could grasp the horrible and dangerous condition they are in, they would be saying to us, "Get me out of this! Do something! Help me!" Can you imagine a lost person in hell saying to a former associate on earth who knew the power of the gospel but did not share it, "Why didn't you tell me? You had a sword, but never tried to cut me loose from the bondage I was in! You had a key to set me free, but you let me remain in captivity!" What suitable answer could a citizen of heaven give to such a resident of earth? How sad when Christians who know the cure for sin can sit in front of television sets laughing, crying, moaning, groaning, yelling, and biting fingernails in response to earthly fantasy. Yet the same individuals can look out on the masses of lost people in the world and feel nothing in response to spiritual reality.

> As he approached Jerusalem and saw the city, he wept over it and said, "If you, even you, had only known on this day what would bring you peace— but now it is hidden from your eyes (Luke 19:41, 42).

> I speak the truth in Christ—I am not lying, my conscience confirms it in the Holy Spirit—I have great sorrow and unceasing anguish in my heart. For I could wish that I myself were cursed and cut off from Christ for the sake of my brothers, those of my own race (Romans 9:1-3).

As citizens of heaven, we have experienced the joy of spiritual deliverance. Jesus has set us free from the power of sin (John 8:31, 32, 36). What must we do to express our gratitude to Him and demonstrate our concern for others who are still in bondage? As concerned missionaries of Jesus residing temporarily on earth, we must act decisively and urgently to free others by finding a way to share the powerful message of salvation in Jesus Christ. We must see and read the invisible sign worn by every lost person. The sign says, "Approach me! Warn me! Tell me! Don't remain silent! Speak up! Plead with me! Provoke me if you must! Do all of this with genuine love and concern— but do it!"

2 To Be Effective as Missionaries for Christ, We Must Be Sure That We Are "Seeing"— Really "Seeing" the Lost People of This World.

20/20 Vision—But Do We Actually "See" the Lost People Around Us?

Many people around us are unsaved—our neighbors, friends, coworkers, and other daily associates. But are we seeing them? We have good vision, but are we seeing lost people with spiritual vision? We are aware of their bodily presence, but do we see their spiritual predicament?

There are different ways of seeing another person. Perhaps a biblical illustration will give clarity to this point. In Luke 10:25-37, Jesus told a great story about a man who was attacked on the road between Jerusalem and Jericho. The man was beaten, robbed, and left to die on the side of the road. There were others who were traveling the same road on this particular day—a Priest, a Levite, and a Samaritan. All three saw the dilemma of this man and recognized that his life was in danger. As you read the account of this incident, pay careful attention to the wording of the text. Specifically, notice how many of the fellow travelers saw the injured man. And then note how many of them *really saw* the man—clearly enough to take action and be helpful. What does it really mean to see another person?

> On one occasion an expert in the law stood up to test Jesus. "Teacher," he asked, "what must I do to inherit eternal life?"
>
> "What is written in the Law?" he replied. "How do you read it?" He answered: " 'Love the Lord your God with all your heart and with all your soul and with all your strength and with all your mind'; and, 'Love your neighbor as yourself.' " "You have answered correctly," Jesus replied. "Do this and you will live." But he wanted to justify himself, so he asked Jesus, "And who is my neighbor?" In reply Jesus said: "A man was going down from Jerusalem to Jericho, when he fell into the hands of robbers. They stripped him of his clothes, beat him and went away, leaving him half dead.
>
> A priest happened to be going down the same road, and when he saw the man, he passed by on the other side.
>
> So too, a Levite, when he came to the place and saw him, passed by on the other side.
>
> But a Samaritan, as he traveled, came where the man was; and when he saw him, he took pity on him.
>
> He went to him and bandaged his wounds, pouring on oil and wine. Then he put the man on his own donkey, took him to an inn and took care of him. The next day he took out two silver coins and gave them to the innkeeper. 'Look after him,' he said, 'and when I return, I will reimburse you for any extra expense you may have.' "Which of these three do you think was a neighbor to the man who fell into the hands of robbers?" The expert in the law replied, "The one who had mercy on him." Jesus told him, "Go and do likewise" (Luke 10:25-37).

The text indicates that there were three travelers who saw one wounded man lying in the ditch. Two of these travelers merely passed by the body of the victim and kept moving without making any effort to assist. Only one fellow traveler actually stopped to give aid and save the man's life. Now a question for us. In a practical and pragmatic way, how many of the three travelers who walked through the crime scene on that day saw—really saw—the wounded man in the ditch? The text says three travelers saw the man, but in a practical sense, there was only one person who actually saw. It was the good Samaritan who paused and paid sacrificially in order to help the wounded stranger.

How many of us as missionaries for Christ in today's culture are seeing—really seeing—the lost people around us? In order to see these needy people, we must have the eyes of Christ. It is with His heart and His eyes that we will be enabled to really see lost people with His love and compassion.

> When Jesus landed and saw a large crowd, he had compassion on them, because they were like sheep without a shepherd. So he began teaching them many things (Mark 6:34).

On a sunny day in the heart of springtime in New York's Central Park, residents were enjoying the beauties of the season—the amazing colors and contrasts. Standing beside the walking path in the park was a blind man. He was seen tapping his cane to attract attention and wearing a sign on his chest, which read—"HELP THE BLIND!" Many people passed by, but few paid attention to him. A little farther down the walking path was another blind beggar who was attracting lots of attention. Almost every passer-by put money in his cup—some would even turn back to make an offering. This man's sign read—"IT'S SPRING TIME, AND I AM BLIND!"

What if we saw every person wearing the invisible sign—"I WANT TO GO TO HEAVEN, BUT I DON'T KNOW HOW! HELP ME"! Jesus saw lost people with great empathy and thus He responded with sacrificial action. Genuine love for people causes us to act—not just talk. Love longs to fill empty places, change wrong directions, heal hurting hearts, and bring cleansing and forgiveness to burdened spirits. Love enables us to see with Jesus' eyes and feel with His heart. We must see—really see the people around us.

3 To Be Effective as Missionaries for Christ, We Must Understand the Scope and Extent of Our Mission to Lost People.

What Is Our Assignment to the Lost People of Earth?

Could there be a misunderstanding about our mission to lost people that needs to be clarified? Could it be that some of us, as citizens of heaven, are confused about our responsibility as missionaries of Jesus on this earth? The consequences are serious because they impact the way we understand our assignment and respond to it. This misunderstanding has resulted in needless frustration, discouragement, guilt, and feelings of failure on the part of many believers.

Precisely, what are our instructions with regard to the lost people of this earth? What does Jesus say we are to do on their behalves? Paraphrased, He said, "Disciples, while you reside on this earth as missionaries for Me, I want you to be involved in the great work of announcing the good news—the gospel—to sinners!" Our task is to announce! Jesus said, "Make sure they hear the message!" Never did the Lord require that we convert every person. Even He was not able to do that. What He did command is that we share the message of hope with everyone.

The word "evangelism" comes from the Greek word, *euangelion*, which means good news. The verb form of this word, *euangelizo*, means to announce good news. The two words are used many times in the New Testament, and are always translated as good news or the action of announcing good news.

So, what is evangelism? What does it mean to evangelize to another individual? To *evangelize* does not mean to *convert*. Evangelism and conversion are two different realities—related, but different. To evangelize to a person means that I have announced the good news—the gospel—to that individual. This person can be evangelized to even if he or she chooses not to be converted. Potentially, it is possible to evangelize to an entire city even if every resident makes the personal choice to reject the gospel. Evangelism is accomplished when the good news is announced even if the goal of evangelism—the conversion of sinners—is not accomplished. In our success-oriented culture, we have tended to confuse the *process* of evangelizing with the *goal* of evangelism.

This distinction can be very liberating for citizens of heaven who are missionaries on earth. It means that we can be successful in the fulfillment of our assignment even if lost people choose to reject our message. Our responsibility is to make sure the people of earth hear the message. It is the responsibility of the hearers to accept or reject that message. Of course, we grieve deeply when unsaved men and women refuse the gospel, while at the same time we can feel a sense of peace and satisfaction knowing that we lovingly shared the good news with them.

Practically, how can this be beneficial? It means that we no longer have to shy away from the work of evangelizing for fear that we might fail. The only way to fail is to withhold the message. So, tell them the good news as well as you are able. But, tell them. Tell them what Jesus has done to save sinners as clearly as possible. But, tell them! Make the message as attractive and appealing as possible. But, share it. Make sure you understand your responsibility. You are not commanded to convert. This is God's job. You are commanded to evangelize. This is our part of the salvation process as the missionaries of Christ on the earth.

> For I have a great sense of obligation to people in both the civilized world and the rest of the world, to the educated and uneducated alike. So I am eager to come to you in Rome, too, to preach the Good News. For I am not ashamed of this Good News about Christ. It is the power of God at work, saving everyone who believes—the Jew first and also the Gentile (Romans 1:14-16 NLT).

4 To Be Effective as Missionaries for Christ, We Must See Evangelism as the Work of All Citizens of Heaven—Not the Work of a Few.

Reaching Out to the Lost—Who Participates in This Work?

With such a big task to carry out, we need a large task force. Evidently, Jesus felt the frustration that comes when there is an abundance of work but a shortage of missionaries.

> Jesus went through all the towns and villages, teaching in their synagogues, preaching the good news of the kingdom and healing every disease and sickness. When he saw the crowds, he had compassion on them, because they were harassed and helpless, like sheep without a shepherd. Then he said to his disciples, "The harvest is plentiful but the workers are few. Ask the Lord of the harvest, therefore, to send out workers into his harvest field" (Matthew 9:35-38).

If the task of reaching lost people is to be done successfully, it will require that every citizen of heaven see himself or herself as a missionary for Christ on earth. Whatever a person's talents or gifts may be, there is a way for each believer to be involved in the broad-based work of evangelism.

In one sense, it takes an entire church to save a soul. Evangelism is a process that involves the proclamation of the good news by words, deeds, attitudes, examples, and lifestyles. Thus, as numerous believers utilize a variety of gifts and talents within the community, lost people are loved, blessed, taught, nurtured, encouraged, and eventually converted. A tasty cherry pie given to an unbeliever who is seeking God must be viewed as a significant evangelistic action. A friendly greeting to an unsaved person is an important evangelistic deed. The greasy tools of a mechanic who volunteers to help a neighbor in need are keys that open big evangelistic doors. A financial gift that makes evangelistic outreach possible is a necessary and helpful component in the overall process of reaching lost people. Every member of the body can have a vital part in the exciting work of extending the love of Christ to the residents of earth.

In fact, those few individuals who have the actual gift of evangelism are, in many cases, only the harvesters. Frequently, there are other believers working behind the scenes who have contributed in significant ways by showing hospitality, extending mercy, teaching lessons, providing funds, giving encouragement—and on and on. The point is that all believers are either planters or waterers, with God being the One who, ultimately, gives the increase. This broader view of evangelism will encourage and motivate many who may now feel unproductive in this area of ministry.

Thus the saying 'One sows and another reaps' is true. I sent you to reap what you have not worked for. Others have done the hard work, and you have reaped the benefits of their labor (John 4:37, 38).

What, after all, is Apollos? And what is Paul? Only servants, through whom you came to believe—as the Lord has assigned to each his task. I planted the seed, Apollos watered it, but God made it grow. So neither he who plants nor he who waters is anything, but only God, who makes things grow. The man who plants and the man who waters have one purpose, and each will be rewarded according to his own labor. For we are God's fellow workers; you are God's field, God's building (1 Corinthians 3:5-9).

5 To Be Effective as Missionaries for Christ, We Must Recognize the Necessity and Value of Relational Evangelism in Today's World.

Relationship Is a Major Key in Today's Evangelism

The vast majority of people in today's world will not be reached by hit-and-run evangelism. Most people must know and trust the messenger before they are willing to embrace the message. Discipleship so often begins with friendship.

Many in the culture today are suspicious of the Christian community. They have seen hypocrisy. They have heard about the scandals. They have smelled our dirty laundry. Constant exposure to humanistic views and values through secular education and the media has not helped our image. Thus, many unbelievers are skeptical, hostile, or even hardened when it comes to what they view as the institutional church and organized religion.

In most cases, this hardening can only be softened over a period of time through warm and genuine relationships. Many people around us are craving intimacy and personal closeness. Many of them have come from broken homes—important relationships have been fractured and personal heartaches have been felt. They want and need a community where they can love and be loved. They want to find an environment where people are real and practice high standards of mutual respect, mutual trust, and mutual servanthood. The colony of heaven on earth—the church—must find practical ways to meet these critical needs. In a community where true Christian love prevails, the atmosphere and culture of heaven is brought to earth. Love within the colony of heaven on earth provides a powerful platform for evangelism.

> "A new command I give you: Love one another. As I have loved you, so you must love one another. By this all men will know that you are my disciples, if you love one another" (John 13:34, 35).

> As apostles of Christ we could have been a burden to you, but we were gentle among you, like a mother caring for her little children. We loved you so much that we were delighted to share with you not only the gospel of God but our lives as well, because you had become so dear to us (1 Thessalonians 2:7, 8).

> "I tell you the truth," Jesus replied, "no one who has left home or brothers or sisters or mother or father or children or fields for me and the gospel will fail to receive a hundred times as much in this present age (homes, brothers, sisters, mothers, children and fields—and with them, persecutions) and in the age to come, eternal life" (Mark 10:29, 30).

We will never win the lost to Jesus by eating their lunch. We may win them if we are willing to show Christian love and take them to lunch. Most surveys will show that the majority of Christians had a believing loved one or friend who shared the good news with them through words and deeds. In today's society, there is a critical need for the quiet work of contagious believers who live redemptively in their daily life as missionaries for Christ. This method worked very well in the first century. Andrew brought Peter to Jesus, and Philip told Nathaniel (John 1:40-42, 45, 46).

Friendship evangelism still works today. Maybe the story of Mamie Adams at the post office helps us understand the relational needs that all humans have. Mamie always bought her stamps at the same post office branch. As she waited in line before the Christmas rush, someone pointed out to her that there was no need to wait in line as there was an automated stamp machine in the lobby. "I know," she said, "but that machine won't ask me about my arthritis." The issue for Mamie was not speed and efficiency. It was human warmth and personal contact. How many Mamie's are there in your neighborhood who are waiting for someone to add the personal touch of genuine concern?

6 To Be Effective as Missionaries for Christ, We Must Teach the Inspired Message of Truth with an Inspiring Spirit of Love.

Truth Must Not Be Sacrificed—and Love Must Not Be Missing.

In Matthew 10:16, Jesus told the men who were going out into the world as His missionaries to be "as innocent as doves." No one has ever been hurt or killed by a dove. We must teach truth, but we must always present the message in love (Ephesians 4:15).

By design, evangelism requires a confrontation between Jesus and sinners—requiring a response. Jesus said, "He who is not with me is against me" (Luke 11:23). Yet as we facilitate this confrontation by teaching the message of truth, we must avoid being needlessly confrontational.

> Don't have anything to do with foolish and stupid arguments, because you know they produce quarrels. And the Lord's servant must not quarrel; instead, he must be kind to everyone, able to teach, not resentful. Those who oppose him he must gently instruct, in the hope that God will grant them repentance leading them to a knowledge of the truth, and that they will come to their senses and escape from the trap of the devil, who has taken them captive to do his will (2 Timothy 2:23-26).

As faithful missionaries for Christ in the world, we can and should use appropriate arguments, but we must not be argumentative. We are to contend for the truth, but we must not be contentious (Jude 1:3). We can be wise without appearing to be wise guys. We can tell people without getting people told. And always, we must be on the offensive without being needlessly offensive.

> Live wisely among those who are not believers, and make the most of every opportunity. Let your conversation be gracious and attractive so that you will have the right response for everyone (Colossians 4:5,6, NLT).

We are fishers of men. You don't catch fish by dropping bombs. As representatives of Jesus on this earth, we not only talk about grace, we also speak with grace. We understand that it is not only important to know the answer, but to know how to answer. "God so loved the world," and so must we.

As it is written, "How beautiful are the feet of those who bring good news!" (Romans 10:15).

FOR FURTHER DISCUSSION AND INTERACTION

1 In any sense, has this study changed your definition and understanding of a missionary for Christ? How many miles must one travel to be a missionary?

2 Using the analogy that Jesus used, how many practical guidelines can you identify to show similarities between fishing for fish and fishing for men?

3 Is it possible that many believers have been unwilling to become involved in the big assignment to evangelize because they have been unwilling to trust Jesus' big promise to provide for them? Evaluate your own position in this matter.

4 At the intellectual level, how real to you is the condition of unsaved people? How real is their danger at an emotional level within you? What can we do within the church to deepen empathy and genuine concern for lost people?

5 How should the Golden Rule (Matthew 7:12) impact the work of evangelism?

6 In this chapter, it was mentioned that lost people wear invisible signs on which they display such messages as, "Speak to me about Jesus! Help me to understand how to be freed from spiritual bondage! Approach me with the gospel!" Based on your observations and personal experiences, what are some of the messages we have put on our signs in response?

7 Why is it difficult for us to see—really see—the unsaved people with whom we rub shoulders daily? How does our modern-day society hinder our desire to speak to others about Jesus Christ?

8 Does the distinction between evangelism and conversion clarify anything for you? In what way has confusion in this area hindered your participation in evangelism?

9 What is your response to the idea that "it takes an entire church to save a soul?" Is it correct to say that the talents and gifts of all believers should be viewed and utilized as tools for evangelistic outreach?

10 Discuss your thoughts and feelings in response to the statement that "most people in today's culture will not be reached by hit-and-run evangelism."

11 What changes would many of us need to make in order to be active participants in friendship evangelism?

12 Jesus said, "Love one another....By this will all men know that you are my disciples if you love one another" (John 13:34, 35). Discuss the implications of disunity and a lack of love among Christians when it comes to effective evangelism.

CHAPTER 11

Be Courageous—
Citizenship Has Its Hardships

Life in a Foreign Country Can Be Difficult

An extended stay in a foreign land can be very trying and stressful. Just ask someone who has walked in these shoes. After the new wears off and the discomfort of culture shock sets in, the only thing that a visiting foreigner may not want to miss is the airplane flight back home.

As Christians, we are citizens of heaven (Philippians 3:20). This world is not our home. As comfortable as we may be, the hard truth is that we do not belong here. The ways of this world are not our ways. The values of this world are not our values. The pleasures of this world can never provide for us the deep-down satisfaction that we crave. To love this world and prefer its treasures and pleasures to the benefits and blessings of our homeland is a sure sign that we are not accepting our true identity as citizens of heaven. Such a mindset could only mean that we are no longer living as pilgrims, but as naturalized citizens of this world.

> So we fix our eyes not on what is seen, but on what is unseen. For what is seen is temporary, but what is unseen is eternal (2 Corinthians 4:18).

> Since, then, you have been raised with Christ, set your hearts on things above, where Christ is seated at the right hand of God. Set your minds on things above, not on earthly things. For you died, and your life is now hidden with Christ in God. When Christ, who is your life, appears, then you also will appear with him in glory (Colossians 3:1-4).

> Do not love the world or anything in the world. If anyone loves the world, the love of the Father is not in him. For everything in the world—the cravings of sinful man, the lust of his eyes and the boasting of what he has and does--comes not from the Father but from the world. The world and its desires pass away, but the man who does the will of God lives forever (1 John 2:15-17).

As we function daily in the earthly realm, our lifestyles are to reflect the spirit of our heavenly homeland. This means that we cannot build our lives around the views and values of this secular world. When people observe our daily walk, there should be obvious signs that, even though we rub shoulders with humanity on earth, our deeper and more defining relationship is with the deity of heaven. Our direction, desires, and decisions are based upon the leadership of heaven rather than the culture of earth. Thus, it should not be uncommon for us to be labeled by the world as nonconformists.

> Do not be yoked together with unbelievers. For what do righteousness and wickedness have in common? Or what fellowship can light have with darkness? What harmony is there between Christ and Belial? What does a believer have in common with an unbeliever? What agreement is there between the temple of God and idols? For we are the temple of the living God. As God has said: "I will live with them and walk among them, and I will be their God, and they will be my people."

> "Therefore come out from them and be separate," says the Lord. "Touch no unclean thing, and I will receive you."

> "I will be a Father to you, and you will be my sons and daughters, says the Lord Almighty."

> Since we have these promises, dear friends, let us purify ourselves from everything that contaminates body and spirit, perfecting holiness out of reverence for God (2 Corinthians 6:14-7:1).

> But among you there must not be even a hint of sexual immorality, or of any kind of impurity, or of greed, because these are improper for God's holy people. Nor should there be obscenity, foolish talk or coarse joking, which are out of place, but rather thanksgiving (Ephesians 5:3, 4).

> For the grace of God has been revealed, bringing salvation to all people. And we are instructed to turn from godless living and sinful pleasures. We should live in this evil world with self-control, right conduct, and devotion to God, while we look forward to that wonderful event when the glory of our great God and Savior, Jesus Christ, will be revealed. He gave his life to free us from every kind of sin, to cleanse us, and to make us his very own people, totally committed to doing what is right (Titus 2:11-14).

As our heavenly views and behaviors collide with those of this world, tension and conflict are inevitable. Nonconformity on the part of Christians has always stirred the ire of those who love darkness and hate the light. Jesus was clear with His disciples on this very point, and the New Testament echoes the same message for us.

"If the world hates you, keep in mind that it hated me first. If you belonged to the world, it would love you as its own. As it is, you do not belong to the world, but I have chosen you out of the world. That is why the world hates you" (John 15:18, 19).

Do not suppose that I have come to bring peace to the earth. I did not come to bring peace, but a sword. For I have come to turn a man against his father, a daughter against her mother, a daughter-in-law against her moth-er-in-law—a man's enemies will be the members of his own household (Matthew 10:34, 36).

You adulterous people, don't you know that friendship with the world is ha-tred toward God? Anyone who chooses to be a friend of the world becomes an enemy of God (James 4:4).

Persecution in the Early Church

For a brief period after the church of Jesus was established on earth, Christians enjoyed the favor of the people around them. Luke, the writer of Acts, describes those days. Speaking about the new converts to Christianity, he said

Every day they continued to meet together in the temple courts. They broke bread in their homes and ate together with glad and sincere hearts, praising God and enjoying the favor of all the people. And the Lord added to their number daily those who were being saved (Acts 2:46, 47).

There were days when the new believers were viewed with favor. But, this could not and would not continue. These good times were short lived. The Christians' devotion to Jesus as Lord and their excitement over their heavenly citizenship were not to be tolerated by the world. Soon, the anger of hostile men began to spread across the Judean countryside like a raging fire. With the stoning of Stephen in Acts 7, the enemies of Christianity set out to viciously exterminate those who dared to wear the name of Jesus Christ.

While they were stoning him, Stephen prayed, "Lord Jesus, receive my spirit." Then he fell on his knees and cried out, "Lord, do not hold this sin against them." When he had said this, he fell asleep. And Saul was there, giving approval to his death. On that day a great persecution broke out against the church at Jerusalem, and all except the apostles were scattered throughout Judea and Samaria. Godly men buried Stephen and mourned deeply for him. But Saul began to destroy the church. Going from house to house, he dragged off men and women and put them in prison. Those who had been scattered preached the Word wherever they went (Acts 7:59-8:4).

Life was anything but easy for these pioneers of the Christian faith. With conviction that they were to be lights in a world of darkness and salt in a world of corruption (Matthew 5:13-16), they courageously moved into the streets of their world determined to uphold and promote a way of life that reflected supreme loyalty to God. However, standing in their path and blocking their way were stubborn and defiant people who were just as determined that these headstrong Christians would not continue to have *their say* and *their way*. These enemies were people who lived their lives without the least regard for the commands of God or the welfare of their fellow men. In Romans, Paul describes the wicked condition of all humans who refuse to live under the authority of God. Quoting from multiple passages in the Old Testament, Paul wrote

"There is no one righteous, not even one;
>there is no one who understands,
>no one who seeks God.
All have turned away,
>they have together become worthless;
>there is no one who does good,
>not even one.
Their throats are open graves;
>their tongues practice deceit.
The poison of vipers is on their lips.
>Their mouths are full of cursing and bitterness.
Their feet are swift to shed blood;
>ruin and misery mark their ways,
>and the way of peace they do not know.
There is no fear of God before their eyes" (Romans 3:10-18).

A collision between two powerful forces was inevitable. People who had no fear of God could not tolerate the God-fearing and God-loving followers of Jesus Christ. The kingdom of light penetrated the world of darkness. The kingdom of God collided with the rule of Satan. Heaven's truth challenged earth's lies. And as Jesus had predicted, His followers faced persecution in many forms—rejection, slander, beatings, torture, imprisonment, and even loss of life. In an effort to encourage the suffering Christians of the first century, the writer of Hebrews reminded them of the horrible conditions believers of other generations had endured.

Some faced jeers and flogging, while still others were chained and put in prison. They were stoned; they were sawed in two; they were put to death by the sword. They went about in sheepskins and goatskins, destitute, persecuted and mistreated—the world was not worthy of them. They wandered in deserts and mountains, and in caves and holes in the ground. These were all commended for their faith, yet none of them received what had been promised. God had planned something better for us so that only together with us would they be made perfect (Hebrews 11:36-40).

How Did the Early Christians Cope with Persecution?

In the heat of battle, believers in the early church did not cave in or renounce their loyalty to Jesus as Lord. In fact, the more their enemies tried to extinguish their fire and fervor, the hotter and brighter they burned for Him.

> We are hard pressed on every side, but not crushed; perplexed, but not in despair; persecuted, but not abandoned; struck down, but not destroyed. We always carry around in our body the death of Jesus, so that the life of Jesus may also be revealed in our body. For we who are alive are always being given over to death for Jesus' sake, so that his life may be revealed in our mortal body (2 Corinthians 4:8-11).

How do you explain the resiliency and courage of the persecuted church? Instead of sinking, they stood. When we would expect them to be acting like victims, they saw themselves as victors. So, what was the spiritual key that enabled them to unlock the steel door of resistance and rejection that the world had slammed in their faces? These amazing people persevered and conquered because of their absolute confidence in the fact that they were citizens of heaven and possessors of enduring possessions that were waiting for them in the life to come.

> Remember those earlier days after you had received the light, when you stood your ground in a great contest in the face of suffering. Sometimes you were publicly exposed to insult and persecution; at other times you stood side by side with those who were so treated. You sympathized with those in prison and joyfully accepted the confiscation of your property, because you knew that you yourselves had better and lasting possessions (Hebrews 10:32-34).

The courageous saints of the first century drew strength from the fact that the Lord Himself had suffered during His sojourn on earth. Wherever the Master leads, the servants must be willing to follow. There was no way for the disciples of Jesus to live as citizens in a place where their Lord had lived as an alien. In fact, for them, to be persecuted for the sake of the gospel was actually counted as an honor and privilege.

> They called the apostles in and had them flogged. Then they ordered them not to speak in the name of Jesus, and let them go. The apostles left the Sanhedrin, rejoicing because they had been counted worthy of suffering disgrace for the Name (Acts 5:40, 41).

Don't Be Surprised When Hardships Come

If you truly follow Christ and walk in His footsteps, you will face resistance or rejection in some form. Much has changed since those early days of New Testament Christianity, but one thing that has not changed is the fact that there are still evil people who persecute those who have the audacity to stand up for the will of God. Citizens of heaven are not loved by residents of earth.

> "I have told you these things, so that in me you may have peace. In this world you will have trouble. But take heart! I have overcome the world" (John 16:33).

> so that no one would be unsettled by these trials. You know quite well that we were destined for them. In fact, when we were with you, we kept telling you that we would be persecuted. And it turned out that way, as you well know (1 Thessalonians 3:3, 4).

> In fact, everyone who wants to live a godly life in Christ Jesus will be persecuted (2 Timothy 3:12).

> Dear friends, do not be surprised at the painful trial you are suffering, as though something strange were happening to you. But rejoice that you participate in the sufferings of Christ, so that you may be overjoyed when his glory is revealed. If you are insulted because of the name of Christ, you are blessed, for the Spirit of glory and of God rests on you. If you suffer, it should not be as a murderer or thief or any other kind of criminal, or even as a meddler. However, if you suffer as a Christian, do not be ashamed, but praise God that you bear that name (1 Peter 4:12-16).

While we should never act foolishly and trigger needless suffering, we can and should expect conflict with those who oppose the kingdom of light. Does not the lengthy and detailed description of the Christian's armor in Ephesians 6:10-18 clearly indicate that Christians should expect conflict with the enemy? Paul's call for all disciples of Jesus to "[p]ut on the full armor of God" (Ephesians 6:11) can only have meaning and relevance in a context of warfare. Why carry a "shield of faith" (v. 16) or "the sword of the Spirit" (v. 17) if there are to be no battles with the forces of darkness? These words should send a clear warning to all Christians: Prepare for conflict!

> Finally, be strong in the Lord and in his mighty power. Put on the full armor of God so that you can take your stand against the devil's schemes. For our struggle is not against flesh and blood, but against the rulers, against the authorities, against the powers of this dark world and against the spiritual forces of evil in the heavenly realms. Therefore put on the full armor of God, so that when the day of evil comes, you may be able to stand your ground, and after you have done everything, to stand. Stand firm then, with the belt of truth buckled around your waist, with the breastplate of righteousness in place, and with your feet fitted with the readiness that comes from the gospel of peace. In addition to all this, take up the shield of faith, with which you can extinguish all the flaming arrows of the evil one. Take the helmet of salvation and the sword of the Spirit, which is the word of God. And pray in the Spirit on all occasions with all kinds of prayers and requests. With this in mind, be alert and always keep on praying for all the saints (Ephesians 6:10-18).

Hardship? Persecution? In America?

Many believers have lived under the delusion that persecution for Christians could never take place in the United States of America. After all, we are protected by the Constitution. We lay claim to First Amendment rights and have no fear of our religious liberties being taken away. Our assumption has been that the founders of this country were God-fearing men who laid the foundation of a nation that would always honor Judeo-Christian principles.

While it is true that the majority of Christians in this country are not being severely persecuted at the present time, it is also true that our culture is rapidly becoming more and more hostile to followers of Jesus. There seems to be an anti-Christian bias that is growing in popularity among many people. Some in positions of influence and leadership are careful to speak positively of and act sympathetically toward other world religions. Yet they are not shy when it comes to belittling, denouncing, and attacking the Christian faith. Things are changing in this country—rapidly. Not many years ago, no one objected to prayer in public arenas. But today in many venues, it is highly suspect, if not forbidden. Once we were one nation under God. Today, we are one nation under—who knows what?

Is it far-fetched to think that the day could come when Christians in America will face severe forms of persecution because of the biblical principles that they practice and the godly standards they promote? In the past, Christians were treated with dignity because of their allegiance to Christ. Is it possible that a day will come when Christians will actually face danger because they wear His name?

Persecution Can Take Many Forms

How do you identify and quantify persecution? In extreme situations, it can result in physical torture, imprisonment, and loss of life. In other forms it is less easy to pinpoint, but it exists just the same. Persecution of the tongue can be just as painful and harmful as persecution of the hand. If you dare to stand firm by biblical standards and Christ-exalting principles, you are likely to feel the rejection of a cultural backlash. There can be social isolation, job loss, financial discrimination, malicious gossip, unfair decisions designed to penalize, or the spreading of false rumors. Persecution can even occur within one's own family. Followers of Christ who stand for truth and resist the lies of this world will, even in America, be reviled and shunned by the enemies of God.

> Blessed are those who are persecuted because of righteousness, for theirs is the kingdom of heaven. Blessed are you when people insult you, persecute you and falsely say all kinds of evil against you because of me. Rejoice and be glad, because great is your reward in heaven, for in the same way they persecuted the prophets who were before you (Matthew 5:10-12).

> Brother will betray brother to death, and a father his child. Children will rebel against their parents and have them put to death. All men will hate you because of me, but he who stands firm to the end will be saved (Mark 13:12, 13).

Why Does Persecution Occur?

When Jesus commissioned His twelve disciples, He painted a clear verbal picture of what they could expect. With no intent to candycoat the danger of their mission to a hostile world, Jesus said

> I am sending you out like sheep among wolves. Therefore be as shrewd as snakes and as innocent as doves (Matthew 10:16).

Sheep in the midst of wolves. This can only mean that God's people are sure to face insult and injury. It is the nature and disposition of a wolf to rip the flesh of a timid and defenseless sheep. Likewise, it is the nature of the world to oppose the children of God. But, can we pinpoint some of the reasons why the world of darkness hates the kingdom of light?

First, Christians are persecuted by the world because they do not conform to the standards that the world embraces. Human beings want other human beings around them to do what they are doing. The rule of the crowd is, "Go with the flow, go along to get along, follow the fashion, and accept the common opinion." The secular world seems to insist that everyone set his or her watch by the town clock. There is resentment toward and rejection of those who dare to embrace different beliefs or live by different standards. Such odd and peculiar people can expect rejection, ridicule, or abuse at the hands of wicked men.

> This is the verdict: Light has come into the world, but men loved darkness instead of light because their deeds were evil. Everyone who does evil hates the light, and will not come into the light for fear that his deeds will be exposed. But whoever lives by the truth comes into the light, so that it may be seen plainly that what he has done has been done through God (John 3:19-21).

> For you have spent enough time in the past doing what pagans choose to do—living in debauchery, lust, drunkenness, orgies, carousing and detestable idolatry. They think it strange that you do not plunge with them into the same flood of dissipation, and they heap abuse on you (1 Peter 4:3, 4).

Devoted disciples of Jesus are not directed by the world's compass as they navigate the journey of life. The arguments, "Everybody does it, everybody will be there, or everybody believes it," are weak and worthless to Christians. Their primary questions are, "What is the will of God? What does the Word of God say?" True followers of Jesus will never accept as right something that God has declared to be wrong.

Second, Christians are persecuted by the world because they dare to confront beliefs and behaviors that are in conflict with the Word of God. The world wants compromise and compliance—not confrontation. This is why Christians in the early church were hated. The position of the apostles was do whatever you must to us, but "we cannot help speaking about what we have seen and heard" (Acts 4: 20). Christians speak up when the world would prefer that they remain silent. Followers of Christ stand up when evil men would prefer that they lay down. Soldiers of Jesus fight when the enemy calls for surrender.

> For you were once darkness, but now you are light in the Lord. Live as children of light (for the fruit of the light consists in all goodness, righteousness

and truth) and find out what pleases the Lord. Have nothing to do with the fruitless deeds of darkness, but rather expose them (Ephesians 5:8-11).

The great dragon was hurled down—that ancient serpent called the devil, or Satan, who leads the whole world astray. He was hurled to the earth, and his angels with him. Then I heard a loud voice in heaven say: "Now have come the salvation and the power and the kingdom of our God, and the authority of his Christ. For the accuser of our brothers, who accuses them before our God day and night, has been hurled down. They overcame him by the blood of the Lamb and by the word of their testimony; they did not love their lives so much as to shrink from death (Revelation 12:9-11).

Third, Christians are persecuted by the world because they are willing to boldly confirm an exclusive message that salvation is experienced and enjoyed only in and through Jesus Christ. If you have a pulse, you have noticed that we are living in the midst of a cultural stampede toward "inclusivism" and "universalism." Most often, these popular words promote the idea that all religions are legitimate paths to deity. You simply select the god, the book, the path, the teacher, the way that best suits your needs and beliefs. Ultimately, they all lead to the same god. There is great reluctance, even a fear today, to speak of the exclusivism of salvation only through Jesus Christ. Understandably, this is offensive to many people. Yet this is clearly and unmistakably what Jesus claimed in His teaching. And this was the conviction of the early church community.

Jesus answered, "I am the way and the truth and the life. No one comes to the Father except through me" (John 14:6).

Salvation is found in no one else, for there is no other name under heaven given to men by which we must be saved (Acts 4:12).

Why is Jesus Christ the only way to God? Because He, alone, is qualified to bridge the gap that exists between the holy and perfect God and humans who are unholy and imperfect. "God is light; in him there is no darkness at all" (1 John 1:5). As sinners who have lived rebelliously before God, we have no right to free access into the presence of the Deity who, in His very nature, is opposed to all that is defiled by sin. We need a qualified mediator who is without flaw or fault to bridge the wide gap between God and us. But who is qualified to serve in this crucial role? Does the human family have a person who is without sin? Only one—Jesus.

God made him [Jesus] who had no sin to be sin for us, so that in him we might become the righteousness of God (2 Corinthians 5:21).

But because Jesus lives forever, he has a permanent priesthood. Therefore he is able to save completely those who come to God through him, because he always lives to intercede for them. Such a high priest meets our need—one who is holy, blameless, pure, set apart from sinners, exalted above the heavens. Unlike the other high priests, he does not need to offer sacrifices day after day, first for his own sins, and then for the sins of the people. He sacrificed for their sins once for all when he offered himself (Hebrews 7:24-27).

Only Jesus is qualified to be our mediator and advocate before God. And how does He prove that He is qualified to be our Savior? The ultimate proof is His empty tomb.

At the place where Jesus was crucified, there was a garden, and in the garden a new tomb, in which no one had ever been laid. Because it was the Jewish day of Preparation and since the tomb was nearby, they laid Jesus there (John 19:41, 42).

On the first day of the week, very early in the morning, the women took the spices they had prepared and went to the tomb. They found the stone rolled away from the tomb, but when they entered, they did not find the body of the Lord Jesus. While they were wondering about this, suddenly two men in clothes that gleamed like lightning stood beside them. In their fright the women bowed down with their faces to the ground, but the men said to them, "Why do you look for the living among the dead? He is not here; he has risen! Remember how he told you, while he was still with you in Galilee: 'The Son of Man must be delivered into the hands of sinful men, be crucified and on the third day be raised again' " (Luke 24:1-7).

We are living in a culture where many are willing to view Jesus as *a way* of salvation, but not *the way*. As citizens of heaven, we must kindly and lovingly help all humans to see that Jesus is the unique Son of God who, alone, can forgive sin and bring us into fellowship and friendship with God.

And this is the testimony: God has given us eternal life, and this life is in his Son. He who has the Son has life; he who does not have the Son of God does not have life (1 John 5:11, 12).

Our Mission to the World and Our Ultimate Victory!

Jesus told us the truth when He said, "In this world, you will have trouble" (John 16:33). When it comes to the conflict between God and Satan, good and evil, or light and darkness, the question is not, "If?" but "When?" trouble is coming. Conflict is inevitable. So, how are we to react and respond when the hardships come? Are we to surrender our convictions and attempt to peacefully coexist with the world? Or are we to attack the world in ugly and unbecoming ways? Should we withdraw from the world and live in isolation? How are we to respond?

While it is true that we are called to be separate from the world (2 Corinthians 6:14-18), it is also true that Jesus sends us into the world to show His love. While hating sin, we are to love sinners and reach out to them with His compassion. The key is to follow the example of Jesus Himself. Rather than angrily rejecting the world, He lovingly moved into it. Though He never sacrificed truth or compromised His heavenly standards, He did lay His life down for the world with a sacrificial spirit. He brought His world of love and light to a world of hatred and darkness. And this is what we must do. His message was, "[T]he Son of Man did not come to be served, but to serve, and to give his life as a ransom for many" (Matthew 20:28).

In the tough times, when resistance is strong and persecution is painful, how are we to view our plight? When writing to suffering Christians who lived in the capital city of Rome and the home of brutal emperors who hated Christians, Paul said, "[W]e face death all day long; we are considered as sheep to be slaughtered. No, in all these things we are more than conquerors" (Romans 8:36, 37). The Greek language is interesting in this passage. The word that meant to be victorious or to conquer was the Greek word *nike*. However, Paul did not just say these persecuted saints were *nike*, he wrote that they would be hyper-*nike*—more than conquerors. The message for all Christians: No matter what the hassles or hardships because of your obedience to Jesus, never forget that ultimately—you win!

FOR FURTHER DISCUSSION AND INTERACTION

1　In the chapter, the point was made that life in a foreign country can be trying and difficult. If we accept the premise that for Christians this world is not our home, why are many of us so comfortable and why do we feel at home?

2　Using examples from current events and news stories, share specific incidents that illustrate why followers of Jesus cannot feel at home in this world.

3　If possible, identify a modern-day Christian who has suffered in the daily workplace because of his or her loyalty to Jesus as Lord. Invite this person to share the circumstances of this experience.

4　Discuss the meaning and application of two key words—relevance and revelation. We want to be relevant as we live in and reach out to the world. Yet we also understand the necessity of living in harmony with God's revelation—His Word. Discuss the tension that must always exist between these two ideas.

5　Why is it difficult for us to assume the role of a nonconformist? What weaknesses and flaws might prompt a Christian to compromise his or her convictions to avoid being labeled as a nonconformist?

6　Frequently, the topic of peer pressure is limited to conversations with young people. How strong is the force of peer pressure among adults?

7　How outlandish is the idea that Christians in America could actually suffer major forms of persecution? Cite examples of places at home and abroad where believers are presently under fire because of their allegiance to Jesus as Lord. (Assign a person to do research in this area.)

8　Severe persecution for Christ sounds so abhorrent to many twenty-first-century believers. How do you explain the fact that Christians in the early church actually rejoiced that they "were counted worthy of suffering disgrace for the Name" (Acts 5:41)?

9　Read Hebrews 10:32-34. What are the practical implications in this passage for us? Make sure to give special emphasis to the last few words in verse 34.

10 As you consider present beliefs and behaviors in the modern American culture, are you optimistic or pessimistic about the spiritual future for our children and grandchildren? How could antagonism toward the Christian faith actually be a blessing and advantage?

11 How will the message of this chapter impact and change your life?

12 As disciples of Jesus, are we viewed by our opponents as hyper-*nike* (more than conquerors)? Explain your response.

CHAPTER 12

Be Encouraged—Citizenship Provides Power for Endurance

Christian Pilgrims Must Go the Distance

We all love to hear stories about people who never give up. Nobody is inspired by the testimony of a quitter. The Bible compares our heavenward pilgrimage to a long distance footrace on a path that is anything but smooth, level, and straight. Sure, there are days when the run is easy—the wind at your back, your course free of obstacles, and your path slanted downhill. But the harsh reality is that there are plenty of days when the run is tough as your rugged path slants uphill and the fierce winds of life hit you in the face. During these hard stretches of the run, some runners grow weary, get discouraged, and decide to quit.

The fact that you began the race is good, but unless you cross the finish line, nothing significant or long lasting is achieved. Jesus said, "[H]e who stands firm to the end will be saved" (Mark 13:13). It's exciting to be in the starting blocks and hear the crack of the gun as the race begins. It's exhilarating to run for a brief time in the big pack of beginners, but if you are to stand with the few finishers in the winner's circle, you must go the distance.

> Enter through the narrow gate. For wide is the gate and broad is the road that leads to destruction, and many enter through it. But small is the gate and narrow the road that leads to life, and only a few find it (Matthew 7:13, 14).

Jesus knew that finishing the Christian race would not be easy. He knew because He endured the pain required of any runner. He wrote the book on how to run and finish the race. At the end of His strenuous mission, He crossed the finish line declaring to His Father, "It is finished" (John 19:30). Our Lord never said to His followers, "You run the grueling race of life, and I'll watch from a celestial cushion in heaven." No, He said, "I'll run first and you can follow My lead." He finished His run. Now He wants to help you successfully complete yours. Never quit. He didn't.

> During the days of Jesus' life on earth, he offered up prayers and petitions with loud cries and tears to the one who could save him from death, and he was heard because of his reverent submission. Although he was a son, he

learned obedience from what he suffered and, once made perfect, he became the source of eternal salvation for all who obey him (Hebrews 5:7-9).

Here's an insightful point for all Christian runners. The Greek word for "race" is *agon*. From this Greek word, we get our English word "agony." What does that word tell you about our endurance race? To begin and finish the Christian race, a person must be prepared to endure agony and exercise discipline.

A farmer went out to sow his seed. As he was scattering the seed, some fell on rock, and when it came up, the plants withered because they had no moisture. Those on the rock are the ones who receive the word with joy when they hear it, but they have no root. They believe for a while, but in the time of testing they fall away (Luke 8:5, 6, 13).

We must go through many hardships to enter the kingdom of God (Acts 14:22).

Let us not become weary in doing good, for at the proper time we will reap a harvest if we do not give up (Galatians 6:9).

If they have escaped the corruption of the world by knowing our Lord and Savior Jesus Christ and are again entangled in it and overcome, they are worse off at the end than they were at the beginning. It would have been better for them not to have known the way of righteousness, than to have known it and then to turn their backs on the sacred command that was passed on to them. Of them the proverbs are true: "A dog returns to its vomit," and, "A sow that is washed goes back to her wallowing in the mud" (2 Peter 2:20-22).

Obviously, the Christian runner needs spiritual stamina. Once you begin this race, it's straight ahead until you take your last breath—no turning back. If you fall along the way—and all of us do—you must get up and keep running. Two postures are in order for Christian runners—we are either up and running, or we are getting back up so that we can continue running. We never stay down. Yes there are times when the path is long, the climb is steep, and the pain is intense; but you must keep moving. Keep going forward—every day—as God gives you strength. We must never quit. There cannot be victory without perseverance.

Stand firm!

Hold on!

Endure!

What Is Christian Endurance?

Endurance is the godly grit and moral tenacity that enables you to hang in as a Christian runner when you would like to bail out. The Greek word for endurance literally means staying power. And, here's the interesting thing about Christian endurance. It is not a passive acceptance that merely tolerates hardships. It is not a "grin and bear it" kind of endurance. No, it is an unbeatable and unbreakable spirit that generates a confidence in God that keeps us actively resisting discouragement and defeat. It is a God-inspired courage that enables us to overcome weakness, hardship, crisis, pain, disappointment—any force, circumstance, condition, person, or thing that might make us want to throw in the towel.

The story about the farmer's old mule illustrates how God-inspired endurance can work for us in the hard times of life. It seems that the animal fell into a dried up well. The farmer decided the mule wasn't worth saving and the well needed filling. So, he called upon his friends and neighbors to bring their shovels and help him fill the hole and bury the old mule. At first, the doomed animal thrashed about, braying and bawling. But after several shovelfuls of dirt, something amazing began to take place. With each scoop of black earth, the mule began to shake off the dirt and step up. In no time at all, the hole was completely filled and the mule stepped out and trotted off into the future.

As runners in the marathon of life, there are days when the secular and sinister world stands on the side of the track of life and flings dirt into our faces. What are we to do? By the strength that God supplies, we must shake the dirt off and step up. The only other option is unacceptable—to lie down and be buried alive. We never quit. Never!

Paul suffered tremendous hardships for the sake of Christ. He was deserted, maligned, imprisoned, beaten, stoned—you name it. But he never gave in or up.

Are they servants of Christ? (I am out of my mind to talk like this.) I am more. I have worked much harder, been in prison more frequently, been flogged more severely, and been exposed to death again and again. Five times I received from the Jews the forty lashes minus one. Three times I was beaten with rods, once I was stoned, three times I was shipwrecked, I spent a night and a day in the open sea. I have been constantly on the move. I have been in danger from rivers, in danger from bandits, in danger from my own countrymen, in danger from Gentiles; in danger in the city, in danger in the country, in danger at sea; and in danger from false brothers. I have labored and toiled and have often gone without sleep; I have known hunger and thirst and have often gone without food; I have been cold and naked. Besides everything else, I face daily the pressure of my concern for all the churches (2 Corinthians 11:23-28).

Knocked Down but Not Knocked Out!

A five-year-old boy walked into a toy shop with his father. The child immediately went up to a giant plastic balloon which looked like a man. The life-size toy was weighted in the feet so that, when he was pushed over, he would pop right back up. The child began to punch the toy man who would go down and then stand up again. This youngster was having the time of his life. The father asked his son, "Why do you think the balloon man keeps getting back up every time you knock him down?" The child looked at the giant balloon and said, "I don't know dad, but I think he is standing up on the inside!"

Jesus wants us to keep standing up on the inside when the circumstances of daily life are pounding us on the outside. One of the greatest passages in the Bible to encourage a faithful run in the race of life is Hebrews 12:1-3. The remainder of this chapter will be devoted to a careful study of this great passage. Christian runner, if you will heed the message of this great text, you will one day stand in the victor's circle and hear Jesus say, "Well done good and faithful servant."

KEY PASSAGE:

Therefore, since we are surrounded by such a great cloud of witnesses, let us throw off everything that hinders and the sin that so easily entangles, and let us run with perseverance the race marked out for us. Let us fix our eyes on Jesus, the author and perfecter of our faith, who for the joy set before him endured the cross, scorning its shame, and sat down at the right hand of the throne of God. Consider him who endured such opposition from sinful men, so that you will not grow weary and lose heart (Hebrews 12:1-3).

A New Testament Book That Says, "Hang In!"

The book of Hebrews was written to Jewish people who had put their faith in Jesus as the Messiah. However, their decision to run the Christian race put them at odds with their fellow countrymen. They were viewed as traitors and heretics. They were accused of betraying their rich heritage. Day in and day out they were harassed and persecuted by their associates. The pressure was so great that many of them were on the verge of dropping out of the race.

Filled with doubt, fear, and confusion, they were about to leave the *grace way* of Jesus and turn back to the *law way* of Moses. They were exhausted and felt that they could not take any more. The letter of Hebrews was written to help these weary runners get their second wind and stay in the race! And, the message of Hebrews will also strengthen and encourage us to keep running and finish the race of faith. Hebrews is an operating manual for our pilgrimage from the foreign land of earth to the homeland of heaven. The message of Hebrews 12:1-3 is

YES, YOU CAN RUN
THE CHRISTIAN RACE SUCCESSFULLY!
AND HERE'S HOW.

1 Remember Other Runners Who Endured

Therefore, since we are surrounded by such a great cloud of witnesses, let us... run... the race...

You can keep running. Look around you. Listen. You are surrounded by the lives and testimonies of numerous men and women of God who never gave up despite hardships that were just as great, or even greater, than the ones you are presently enduring. They didn't quit, and you must not either.

Many of these faithful men and women who successfully finished the race of eternal life are mentioned by name in Hebrews 11, which serves as the broader context for our key passage in Hebrews 12. These Old Testament witnesses are shouting to you through the Scriptures to keep running your race to the very end. Hear them!

Listen! You can hear the encouraging voice of Abel who still speaks even though he is dead (Hebrews 11:4.) Through the Scriptures, Abel says to you, "Hey, what do you mean you're thinking about quitting? No way! I remained faithful to God even though I was hated and put to death by my own brother. You can't quit. You must keep running—no matter what!"

Listen! You can hear the testimony of Noah as he speaks through the Word of God. He says to you, "Get up and keep going! Sure it's difficult, but you must not be a quitter. My peers laughed at and ridiculed me for years as I built that boat in the middle of a desert. The insults were hard to bear and the pressure was great, but God gave me strength to endure. And, He will do the same for you. You get up! Keep running!"

Listen! You can hear the voices of other Old Testament saints mentioned in Hebrews 11—Abraham, Moses, the folks who marched around Jericho, Rahab, Gideon, David, Samuel, the prophets, and others—people who never gave in or up. "What do you mean you're quitting"? These people "were tortured and refused to be released....Some faced jeers and flogging, while still others were chained and put in prison. They were stoned; they were sawed in two; they were put to death by the sword. They went about in sheepskins and goatskins, destitute, persecuted and mistreated—the world was not worthy of them. They wandered in deserts and mountains, and in caves and holes in the ground" (Hebrews 11:35-38). If they endured, you can too. Keep running!

Listen! You can hear the testimony of Paul in the New Testament. He was slandered, beaten, stoned, imprisoned, and rejected. In fact, he says to you, "We were under great pressure, far beyond our ability to endure, so that we despaired even of life. Indeed, in our hearts we felt the sentence of death. But this happened that we might not rely on ourselves but on God, who raises the dead. He has delivered us from such a deadly peril, and he will deliver [you]. On him, we have set our hope that he will continue to deliver us." (2 Corinthians 1:8-10). To you, weary runner, Paul would say, "Keep running! God will give you the strength to clear the hurdles and carry the burdens. Run the race of faith to the very end. Yes, you can finish because God will give you the strength!"

Think about it! The footprints of many faithful pilgrims from the past have been left on the pathway for us to observe. And when you take the time to carefully study the footprints of the resilient travelers who walked ahead of us, it is easy to see that they all point in one direction—heavenward. None point in a backward direction. None point to the side or off the track completely. Just straight ahead toward the final goal. And when you bend down to examine the footprints more closely, you can see blood stains and sweat droplets left by those determined men and women. Many of the faithful pilgrims who ran before us were under terrific pressure from their opponents and opted to die for their God rather than to live for their own comforts. So do as they did and keep walking. Don't look back. Keep your footprints pointed in the direction of home. Stay the course. You are traveling in good company.

Let's add one additional thought that is so crucial. The Hebrew writer says to Christians who are beaten down and battered, "[L]et us run...the race" (Hebrews 12:1). We are in this race together. In a sense, we are running in company with faithful people of all ages. Yes, we are running with Abraham, Isaac, Jacob, and others from the Old Testament days. And we are running with Peter, James, John, and other great saints who ran during the early days of the New Testament period. And don't forget that we are running with Tom, Dick, and Harriett in our own day—other believers who are our fellow travelers. We must stick together. We must gain strength by sharing our mutual lifestyles of obedience. We need each other. Let's run in a caravan so that we encourage, exhort, and help each other all along the way. "Let us run...the race."

2 Get Rid of Every Hindrance and Sin That Entangles

...let us throw off everything that hinders and the sin that so easily entangles...

Personal discipline is necessary to excel at anything. This applies to running a race. You don't wake up one morning and suddenly decide to enter a marathon. At the starting blocks of a long-distance race, you'll not find overweight, potbellied runners. Before the run, great preparations are made as participants devote themselves to sacrificial training, conditioning, and dieting. Every ounce of excess weight is taken off. Competitors understand the importance of approaching the starting line slim and trim. As they move onto the track, you will see them stripping away every piece of unnecessary clothing or anything else that might be a hindrance. Serious runners never wear bulky overcoats or boots. You never see backpacks and water jugs being carried by runners. They know the importance of running light and lean.

In the race of life, we are to throw off everything that hinders. Anything—even something that is not inherently evil—can be a hindrance. As necessary as it is to have a job, there are some jobs that become so demanding that they hinder our efforts to run in the Christian race. There are relationships, hobbies, and pleasures that are not sinful in themselves, yet they weigh us down—they scramble our priorities, pollute our values, dilute our zeal, and distract our attention. They drain our energy and use up our time. Hindrances are as individual as the person. Anything that distracts our focus, weakens our resolve, retards our speed, or impedes our progress is a weight or hindrance. This means that to run a good race, we must commit ourselves to a life of Christian discipline.

A farmer once killed a huge eagle with a wing span of seven feet. He was amazed that he was able to get close enough to this huge bird to kill it. After the kill, he approached the bird and discovered why it had not escaped. He found a steel trap attached to the bird's leg. The trap had not killed the eagle, but it did weigh the bird down so that flying was extremely difficult. With the additional weight of that trap attached to its leg, the bird's efficiency was lowered and its strength was depleted. The trap did not kill the bird, but its weight did weaken the bird's ability to soar and survive. What is it in your life that is weighing you down and lowering your efficiency as a Christian runner?

"Everything is permissible for me"—but not everything is beneficial. "Everything is permissible for me"—but I will not be mastered by anything (1 Corinthians 6:12).

And then, of course, the Hebrew writer mentions the need for a Christian runner to throw off sin. To live in willful disobedience to God straps you with guilt and shame that can feel like heavy weights tied around your neck. Guilt is awful. It creates spiritual, emotional, mental, and physical pain (Psalm 32:3-5; 38:1-22). Have you been there? No one can successfully complete the trek of life loaded down with such burdens. The Hebrew writer says, "Let us throw off the sin that so easily entangles." This does not mean that you are out of the race if you commit sin. Otherwise, we would all be disqualified. It does mean that you cannot run a successful race and win the prize if, because of compromise and rationalization, you continue to hold on to beliefs and behaviors that God labels as destructive and evil.

You can't successfully run in the race of Christian purity while wearing the overcoat of sexual immorality. Come on! You won't last in the race of daily dependency on God if you are carrying suitcases filled with your money, portfolios, and deeds of trust. Don't kid yourself! You'll fail as a runner if the heavy weights of sinful addictions are strapped to your legs. And if you are really serious about running the race of Christian obedience, you'll have to take off that heavy helmet of stubbornness and self-will. David, the psalmist, describes the damaging effects of sin—"My guilt has overwhelmed me, like a burden too heavy to bear" (Psalm 38:4).

3 Run with Perseverance the Race Marked Out for Us

...and let us run with perseverance the race marked out for us...

The Christian race is marked out for us. As runners, we don't arbitrarily decide on the length and limits of our course. The boundaries and borders have been determined by the Pacesetter, Jesus Christ. Our only option is to run according to His terms. Can you imagine a race where everybody makes up their own rules and their own boundaries as they go? We do have a choice as to whether or not to enter the race. And, we decide how long to stay in the race. But once we commit to run, we must then submit ourselves fully to the authority of the Race Master, Jesus Christ.

Then Jesus came to them and said, "All authority in heaven and on earth has been given to me. Therefore go and make disciples of all nations, baptizing them in the name of the Father and of the Son and of the Holy Spirit, and teaching them to obey everything I have commanded you. And surely I am with you always, to the very end of the age" (Matthew 28:18-20).

Similarly, if anyone competes as an athlete, he does not receive the victor's crown unless he competes according to the rules (2 Timothy 2:5).

Not only must we run according to the will of God, but we must run with perseverance. The Duke of Wellington returned to England after defeating Napoleon at Waterloo. He and his men were being praised for their courage and perseverance in defeating Napoleon and his army. The Duke said, "The army of Napoleon were men of courage, but my men had five minutes more courage and perseverance than Napoleon's men. And that is what brought us victory." Just five more minutes of not quitting made the difference.

In the parable of the sower, Jesus says, "But the seed on good soil stands for those with a noble and good heart, who hear the word, retain it, and by persevering produce a crop" (Luke 8:15). To merely hear the Word is not sufficient. You must hear, retain, and persevere! When you are tired and tempted to slow down or quit, you have to do what every other successful runner has done. Exercise holy determination. That's Christian endurance. You lean hard on God's strength and keep on walking in obedience when you are tempted to lose heart. No matter what the conditions, you don't quit!

You need to persevere so that when you have done the will of God, you will receive what he has promised (Hebrews 10:36).

Then Jesus told his disciples a parable to show them that they should always pray and not give up. He said: "In a certain town there was a judge who neither feared God nor cared about men. And there was a widow in that town who kept coming to him with the plea, 'Grant me justice against my adversary.' For some time he refused. But finally he said to himself, 'Even though I don't fear God or care about men, yet because this widow keeps bothering me, I will see that she gets justice, so that she won't eventually wear me out with her coming!'" And the Lord said, "Listen to what the unjust judge says. And will not God bring about justice for his chosen ones, who cry out to him day and night? Will he keep putting them off? I tell you, he will see that they get justice, and quickly. However, when the Son of Man comes, will he find faith on the earth?" (Luke 18:1-8).

Not only so, but we also rejoice in our sufferings, because we know that suffering produces perseverance; perseverance, character; and character, hope (Romans 5:3, 4).

Consider it pure joy, my brothers, whenever you face trials of many kinds, because you know that the testing of your faith develops perseverance. Perseverance must finish its work so that you may be mature and complete, not lacking anything. If any of you lacks wisdom, he should ask God, who gives generously to all without finding fault, and it will be given to him (James 1:2-5).

To the angel of the church in Ephesus write: These are the words of him who holds the seven stars in his right hand and walks among the seven golden lampstands: I know your deeds, your hard work and your perseverance. I know that you cannot tolerate wicked men, that you have tested those who claim to be apostles but are not, and have found them false. You have persevered and have endured hardships for my name, and have not grown weary (Revelation 2:1-3).

Experienced runners know that once you are on the track, the biggest secret for success is perseverance. So it is in the race of eternal life. Perseverance is that grit and stamina that keeps you hanging in five more minutes and one more day—it's resolving daily to live with a holy determination. When you are winded, wounded, or weary, holy determination will keep you on your feet or keep you getting back up on your feet if you've fallen. Finishers in the race of life are those who persevere even in the midst of tough and trying circumstances. Always remember, Christian pilgrim, you are not defeated until you give up.

Jesus said, "To him who overcomes, I will give the right to eat from the tree of life, which is in the paradise of God" (Revelation 2:7).

4 Fix Your Eyes on Jesus Throughout the Race

Let us fix our eyes on Jesus, the author and perfecter of our faith, who for the joy set before him endured the cross, scorning its shame, and sat down at the right hand of the throne of God (Hebrews 12:2).

I don't know who said it, but it's true. In the race of life, you must make sure that you keep "the Son" in your eyes at all times. You will stumble and fall if you get distracted and fail to maintain a focus on Jesus. It's not enough to glance in His direction now and then. You must maintain a continual fixation on Him. We're talking here about the power of trusting and obedient faith.

Faith is the key to a successful run in the race of life. But who is "the author and perfecter of our faith" (Hebrews 12:2)? Jesus. The original word for author suggests such concepts as leader, founder, and pioneer. The term was used for those who cut a path for their followers. And He is the perfecter of our faith. The original word for perfecter speaks of one who has reached the highest level of faith in his own life. He has already done what we are now in the process of doing—running in the race of life with trusting and obedient faith. Thus, from the starting blocks all the way to the finish line, your chief assignment is to keep your eyes fixed and focused on Jesus.

There was a British soldier in World War I who lost heart for the battle and deserted. Trying to reach the coast for a boat to England, he ended up wandering in the pitch black night, hopelessly lost. In the darkness, he came across what he thought was a signpost. It was so dark that he began to climb the post so that he could read it and, hopefully, identify his location. As he reached the top of the pole, he struck a match for light to read the sign. As the image became visible, he found himself looking squarely into the face of Jesus Christ. He realized that, rather than running into a signpost, he had climbed a roadside crucifix. Later, as this soldier told someone of this experience, he said, "Clinging to the top of that sign post, I suddenly remembered the One who had died for me—who had endured hardship on my behalf yet had never turned back. The next morning I was back in the trenches." We, too, are in a battle. We must not defect. The key is to keep your eyes on Jesus.

In another Hebrew passage, as the writer was battling to keep weak and wavering saints in the Christian race, he said, "Therefore, holy brothers, who share in the heavenly calling, fix your thoughts on Jesus, the apostle and high priest whom we confess" (Hebrews 3:1). The word translated "fix" means to observe thoughtfully and consider carefully. In fact, it's the idea of having a fixed gaze that looks away from everything else. Faith in Jesus Christ is the key to winning the race for eternal life.

As we apply these words about staying focused on Jesus, don't forget Peter's experience in Matthew 14:25-33. Take a moment to read those verses again. This man was actually walking on water as long as he looked to Jesus in faith. Only when he looked away from Jesus and focused on the frightening conditions around him did Peter begin to suck water instead of air. There are many reasons as to why we must keep our eyes fixed on Jesus.

First, keep your eyes on Jesus because He is the One who continually keeps you forgiven and free from the guilt and shame of sin. You can't run a good race if you are dragging around the heavy guilt of your past or the painful failures of your present. These burdens will wear you down quickly.

Truth be told, we still are a mess before God—even as believers. Are we not still fighting a battle with our flesh? For example, is telling the truth not a struggle at times? Is it not still difficult to resist the temptation to lust? How easy is it, even as a believer, for you to eliminate resentment, bitterness, anger, and hatred from your heart? And how well are you doing in the area of maintaining joy and contentment even when the circumstances of your life are painful and heavy to bear? Can we accept the fact that human weaknesses and struggles are going to be with us for the entire journey homeward?

But again, we never quit! With our eyes on Jesus, the One who was rejected, spit upon, beaten, and put to death, we continue to run the race every day. The adversary keeps coming back, but we keep on resisting. When we fall, we get up and run again because of our faith in Jesus Christ. We are climbers on the mountain of holiness. We gradually scale this peak with holy determination because we know that, by the grace of God, it is as if we were already at the summit standing in victory (Hebrews 10:14). We are slowly and painfully becoming what God has already made us by grace—holy. Day by day, we are learning to lean on the power of the Holy Spirit as we resist the drag of our flesh (Romans 8:5-17; Galatians 5:16-25). We are in the race of faith, and endurance will be required until we cross over into the heavenly homeland.

But, be encouraged. As a citizen of heaven, you have the means to persevere and finish your run successfully. The sure sign that you are making the heavenward journey in faith is the fact that you are choosing day by day to stay in the race. No turning back. No dropping out. The adversary tries to discourage you, but you continue to resist and run—looking to the Savior. Even when you fall, you learn and grow from the experience. Your falls along the path only make you more determined to get up and run again. Maybe you feel that you have little to show for your faith. Is someone saying, "I have never built a boat like Noah? I have never sacrificed like Abraham. I have never been thrown into a den of lions like Daniel." It is true that different runners encounter different experiences along the way. But, be encouraged! The good word for all runners is, "[H[e who stands firm [endures] to the end will be saved" (Mark 13:13). If you are still living by faith when you die, you are promised the same victory with all other successful runners. Your goal must be to keep your eyes focused on your great Savior rather than on your gross sins.

> All these people were still living by faith when they died. They did not receive the things promised; they only saw them and welcomed them from a distance. And they admitted that they were aliens and strangers on earth. People who say such things show that they are looking for a country of their own. If they had been thinking of the country they had left, they would have had opportunity to return. Instead, they were longing for a better country—a heavenly one. Therefore God is not ashamed to be called their God, for he has prepared a city for them (Hebrews 11:13-16).

Members of Alcohol's Anonymous begin every public testimony with the statement, "My name is _____ and I am an alcoholic." As runners in the race of life, we can all say, "My name is _____ and I am a sinner." But this is far from where our testimony ends. Quickly, we add, "Even though I am a sinner, my eyes are fixed and focused on the One who became sin for me and the One who gives me His righteousness as a gift of grace. In Him, I am not condemned! I am saved by the blood that He shed for me at Calvary (2 Corinthians 5:21; Romans 8:1; 1 John 5:11-13).

Sure, our sins—past, present, and future—are very serious, but because of God's mercy and our trusting faith in Jesus, the guilt and penalty of our sins have been buried in the ocean of God's amazing grace. This is the gospel—the good news! Do you believe it? Will you apply it emotionally? You cannot focus on your sins and run a successful race. You must remain fixed and focused on your Savior. The words of an old song say it beautifully.

I heard the voice of Jesus say,
"I am this dark world's light;
Look unto Me, Thy morn shall rise,
And all Thy day be bright."
I looked to Jesus, and I found
In Him my Star, my Sun;
And in that Light of life I'll walk
Till traveling days are done.

—*Horatius Bonar, 1846*

Second, keep your eyes on Jesus because He is your primary source for daily strength, comfort, and hope as you make the difficult pilgrimage toward home. With eyes of faith, can you see Jesus at this moment sitting at the right hand of God calling your name and serving as your intercessor and advocate (Romans 8:34; 1 Timothy 2:5, 6; 1 John 2:1, 2)? Consider the fact that He pleads for you and watches over your interests with an eye that never sleeps. His communication line is never busy, and His door is always open. Morning, noon, and night He is ready to hear your cries, to sympathize with your weaknesses, to give you wisdom as you make decisions, to strengthen you in your trials, and to bring you safely home. He never forgets you, and He always loves you. Look to Him for your salvation; then keep a fixed gaze upon Him for the daily strength and courage you need to live as a stranger in this world. If you keep your eyes fixed on Jesus, you are guaranteed a special place in the winners' circle of the race of faith. Like Moses and all other runners in the race, you must have eyes of faith to see the invisible (Hebrews 11:1, 27).

He gives strength to the weary and increases the power of the weak. Even youths grow tired and weary, and young men stumble and fall; but those who hope in the LORD will renew their strength. They will soar on wings like eagles; they will run and not grow weary, they will walk and not be faint (Isaiah 40:29-31).

For I am already being poured out like a drink offering, and the time has come for my departure. I have fought the good fight, I have finished the race, I have kept the faith. Now there is in store for me the crown of righteousness, which the Lord, the righteous Judge, will award to me on that day—and not only to me, but also to all who have longed for his appearing (2 Timothy 4:6-8).

5 Do Not Grow Weary and Lose Heart—FINISH!

Consider him who endured such opposition from sinful men, so that you will not grow weary and lose heart (Hebrews 12:3).

What is your burden? What sorrow are you carrying? What heavy load is making it hard for you to run well in the race of life? Have you lost a dear loved one? Have people disappointed you? Has health failed you? Have setbacks caused you to feel down and defeated? Are you perplexed by the twists and turns that you have encountered on the pathway of life? The solution? "Consider him who endured such opposition from sinful men, so that you will not grow weary and lose heart."

If you are feeling weak, weary, and disheartened, take another long look at the faith of Jesus. The Hebrew writer uses a banking term to say, "Calculate and take inventory of how Jesus endured disappointment, discouragement, and cruelty at the hands of His enemies." Do you believe that you are at the end of your own power? Don't lose heart! You may be feeling that your wounds are so deep, your burdens so heavy, and your difficulties so great. But please remember and believe that Jesus, your Savior, friend, and brother, is the Lord Almighty. He can and will perfect His strength in your weakness. He will provide healing for your wounds, He will get under your burdens with you, and He will help you to cope with your difficulties. Look to Jesus and hide behind the shield of His almightiness. Press on dear pilgrim.

To keep me from becoming conceited because of these surpassingly great revelations, there was given me a thorn in my flesh, a messenger of Satan, to torment me. Three times I pleaded with the Lord to take it away from me. But he said to me, "My grace is sufficient for you, for my power is made perfect in weakness." Therefore I will boast all the more gladly about my weaknesses, so that Christ's power may rest on me. That is why, for

Christ's sake, I delight in weaknesses, in insults, in hardships, in persecutions, in difficulties. For when I am weak, then I am strong (2 Corinthians 12:7-10).

We must persevere! If we don't bear the cross, we cannot wear the crown. But "if we endure, we shall also reign with Him" (2 Timothy 2:12) There is no legitimate reason to give in or quit. Better days are coming. God is faithful! He will keep His promises. The victory circle awaits you. Be patient, weary pilgrim! Every day you are getting closer to paradise. The best is yet to come!

FOR FURTHER DISCUSSION AND INTERACTION

1 When you became a Christian, how well did you understand the commitment that you were making? In our efforts to reach lost people, are we doing an adequate job in helping them to understand the challenge they are accepting and the difficult path they are entering? Are we more concerned about the quantity of disciples than the quality of disciples? Are we helping potential converts to count the cost?

2 For you, what is the toughest test in living every day for Jesus Christ in today's world? Shouldn't we be sharing our struggles with each other so that we can pray for and encourage one another? Why are we not talking with each other about such realities? Is there anyone in your group who would like to ask for prayer about a particular struggle going on in his or her life at the present time?

3 The Greek word for path is *agon*—the word from which we get our English word "agony." From your vantage point as a Christian runner, does "the path" of life for Christians involve agony? This would be a good time for mature runners to speak to new runners about the agony that they may encounter along the path of life. We don't have to be pessimistic, but we do need to be realistic about the Christian race.

4 In every period of time, the Christian race has always been a challenge—not easy. What conditions or circumstances can you identify that may make running especially challenging and difficult in our day and in our culture?

5 In an environment where great emphasis is given to pluralism, inclusiveness, and tolerance, how do you feel about the assertion that only a few (Matthew 7:13-14) will be privileged to stand in the winner's circle when the race of life is over?

6 Ask a mature believer to openly share five beliefs or behaviors that have enabled him or her to cope with the hardships of life and endure up until the present time as a runner on the path of life.

7 What Old or New Testament character, more than any other, encourages you to fight off discouragement and keep on running the Christian race? Why?

8 Within your local fellowship, are Christian pilgrims making the heaven-ward journey in a caravan? Why is it risky to run solo in this grueling race? What can we do to improve in this area?

9 Identify three practical steps that most every Christian could take to throw off some of the foremost hindrances that slow us down in the race of life.

10 How would you describe the major reason as to why we are unwilling to throw off the sin that so easily entangles us as we attempt to run the Christian race?

11 Why is it hard for us to accept our acceptance? Why is it difficult for us to know, without doubt, that we are in friendship and fellowship with God even though we continue to struggle and stumble as runners in the race of life?

12 If possible, find a Christian or group of believers who know and will sing the song, "Turn Your Eyes Upon Jesus." The words of this song capture the purpose of this lesson. Or, sing this great song yourself. Let its message penetrate your heart.

13 Take time to let members of your group tell why they feel refreshed and re-energized to keep on running in the race of life in spite of hardships. Let each testimony begin with the words, "I resolve to keep running in the race of faith because..."

14 Faith is being sure and certain about realities you cannot see. Discuss why faith is so crucial if we are to be winners in the race of life. In your discussion, refer to Paul's words in 2 Corinthians 4:16-18.

CHAPTER 13

Be Faithful to the End— We'll Be Going Home Soon

I Want to Go Home!

As fun as it is to travel to foreign places, there's no place like home.

Most of us have found ourselves in a situation where we wanted to go home. Some may have actually experienced homesickness. It's awful. There is an aching, empty feeling of being in one place, but longing for another. When you are sick for home, nothing around you can fill up that empty place inside.

After spending time—even pleasurable time—as a visitor in a foreign country, it is not uncommon for a traveler to feel an excitement and eagerness about packing up and going home. Every time I have traveled to a distant place, regardless of how enjoyable the trip may have been, I have always looked forward to that day when my journey would turn in a homeward direction—the land of my birth and the dwelling place of my loved ones. "Going home" are words that have great appeal to most of us.

Home. There's just no place like it. It's never altogether perfect because fallible humans live there, but it's still home. It's where your family is. It's where you are comfortable—the place where you are wanted, accepted, loved, and protected. Home is where you belong. It's a refuge from the world. More and more as I get older, I find myself longing and loving to go home.

God Provided a Wonderful Home for Mankind

Representatively through Adam and Eve, all of mankind once lived in the Garden of Eden. This paradise was designed by God to be a perfect and permanent home for the first couple and their descendants. That includes us. Yes, Eden was created by God to be your eternal home and mine.

If you read the Scriptures and use your imagination, you can do a quick virtual tour of that beautiful garden-home. Can you visualize the scene? Picture a stunning territory where rivers flowed; where trees, flowers, vegetables, and grasses grew; and where birds, animals, and fish lived in peaceful coexistence with human beings. All needs were provided for in abundant supply. In that wonderful environment, humans were given dominion. They were allowed to rule over God's creation (Genesis 1:28-30). What a dream home!

On your virtual Eden tour, visualize an amazing tree that grows in the middle of this garden. God labeled it the tree of life (Genesis 2:9). To Adam and Eve, God said, "Eat freely from this tree! Enjoy!" And, as long as they did, there was no sickness, aging, or death. Wow! What a home! No park or garden that man has ever made compares with our original homeplace in Eden.

But, you know the rest of the sad story. Adam and Eve blew it! They willfully disobeyed God by eating from the one tree that was forbidden, the tree of the knowledge of good and evil. They sinned. This led to a complete disruption of the peace and permanence of our original homeplace. Adam and Eve broke their Father's heart and everything changed. Paradise was lost. They were driven out of their garden-home and forced to live in a world that was filled with trials and tribulations. When they made their shameful exit from Eden, we left with them—representatively. And from the time of this terrible expulsion, humans have longed and yearned to live again in a peaceful, permanent, and perfect environment like Eden. We want to go to our forever home.

In Heaven—an Eden-Like Environment Will Be Restored

Heaven is the promised, perfect, and permanent home that we desire and need. According to the Bible, what we lost when we were driven out of the gates of Eden we are going to regain when we are welcomed at the entryway of heaven. Just think! Every day at 12:01 A.M., we are one day closer to a grand entry into our eternal home! The words of the writer of Hebrews ring in our ears and resonate in our hearts, "[H]ere we do not have an enduring city, but we are looking for the city that is to come" (Hebrews 13:14). We are on our way home—we are going to our Father's house. Home sweet home.

For most humans, the appeal of the heavenly homeland increases significantly when life on earth gets hard and heavy. Are you there yet? For example, think about the slaves who lived in the 1800s. After long hours in the sweltering cotton fields, they would gather at night to sing about a home where they would enjoy benefits that, they believed, this world would never provide—rest, peace, and freedom. Wallis Willis, a slave sometime prior to 1862, composed that familiar spiritual, "Swing Low Sweet Chariot." Inspired by the biblical account of Elijah's ascension into heaven by a chariot, Willis wrote, "Swing low sweet chariot, coming for to carry me home."

Even though you and I are not the victims of social slavery, we do, at times, face painful circumstances that intensify our yearning for the rest, peace, and freedom of heaven. Trials and tears are very much a part of our lives in this world. Look around. Perhaps, the most pervasive and visible characteristic of life in the flesh is sorrow. There are burdensome circumstances, broken relationships, and bitter regrets, all of which point to bewildered people who, in their hearts, are still singing or saying in some fashion, "Swing low, sweet chariot. Come and take me home." The pain that we feel in this world continues to stir a deep longing for the painless homeland of heaven.

> I consider that our present sufferings are not worth comparing with the glory that will be revealed in us (Romans 8:18).

I read about a large church building that had a huge arch over the pulpit, which was lined with sixty-six electric lights. Each light represented one book of the Bible. These lights were always kept shining during the sermon. One night the preacher was delivering his sermon while his young son sat in one of the front pews. The father noticed that his son was restless and was trying hard to attract his attention. Finally, the speaker stopped in the middle of his sermon and said, "Well, what is it, son?" Instantly, pointing at one of the sixty-six lights, he said, "Daddy, Lamentations is out!" The words of this young lad point to a day of hope for us. While we live in this world, we have lamentations (grief, weeping, wailing), but one day, "lamentations will be out" because we will finally reside in the problem-free homeland of heaven.

In This World, We Are Away from the Lord

In 2 Corinthians 5, Paul describes life in the physical body as being "away from the Lord." Of course, the Lord is with us, even now, in a spiritual sense—He walks beside us daily. However, He is not with us now as He will be when we vacate these physical bodies and enjoy a much greater dimension of His presence in the beautiful homeland of heaven. In that heavenly setting, we will experience visible, verbal, and emotional connections with our Lord that are not available to us while we are at home in the body. And when those exciting conditions become realities for us, Paul says that we will really be "at home with the Lord." Also, notice in the verses that follow that Paul describes this future condition as "our preference":

> For while we are in this tent, we groan and are burdened, because we do not wish to be unclothed but to be clothed with our heavenly dwelling, so that what is mortal may be swallowed up by life. Now it is God who has made us for this very purpose and has given us the Spirit as a deposit, guaranteeing what is to come. Therefore we are always confident and know that as long as we are at home in the body we are away from the Lord. We live by faith, not by sight. We are confident, I say, and would prefer to be away from the body and at home with the Lord (2 Corinthians 5:4-8).

I Can't Feel at Home in This World Anymore

As beautiful and inviting as this present world can be, there are many things in it that continually remind us that it is not home. Oh, we work hard to make it feel like home. But just about the time we get comfortable and cozy, the harsh realities of this fallen world rudely and painfully interrupt. Suddenly, our castles are destroyed, our capital is depleted, our celebrations are dampened, and our control is disrupted. Again and again, the biblical message is confirmed. We live in this world as aliens and strangers. No matter how many years we reside in this land, deep down inside, it never quite feels like home.

Our permanent and primary citizenship is not in this world. Even though I have an official passport that declares me a citizen of the United States, the reality is that, as a Christian, my primary and permanent citizenship is in heaven.

> But our citizenship is in heaven. And we eagerly await a Savior from there, the Lord Jesus Christ (Philippians 3:20).

> Since you call on a Father who judges each man's work impartially, live your lives as strangers here in reverent fear (1 Peter 1:17).

> Dear friends, I urge you, as aliens and strangers in the world, to abstain from sinful desires, which war against your soul (1 Peter 2:11).

Pay careful attention to the words used in these verses to describe our lives in this world. *Aliens* are people who reside in one place, but have citizenship in another. *Strangers* are outsiders who practice a different culture, speak with a different sound, and embrace different views and values. Living in a strange land, these people find it difficult to fit in. More and more, many of us are discovering that we feel less and less at home in this world. Only when we finally enter the homeland of heaven will we really be able to say, "Ah, home at last!"

A letter to Diognetus, written at the end of the fourth century, plainly describes the status of Christians then and now:

> Christians are indistinguishable from other men either by nationality, language or customs. They do not inhabit separate cities of their own, or speak a strange dialect, or follow some outlandish way of life....With regard to dress, food and manner of life in general, they follow the customs of whatever city they happen to be living in, whether it is Greek or foreign.

And yet there is something extraordinary about their lives. They live in their own countries as though they were only passing through. They play their full role as citizens, but labor under all the disabilities of aliens. Any country can be their homeland, but for them their homeland, wherever it may be, is a foreign country....They pass their days upon earth, but they are citizens of heaven.

As crazy as it may sound to a secular-minded person, the fact is that, as Christians, we are, in a sense, homeless. And because we are temporary residents of this world, we refuse to foolishly act like travelers, who spend a week in a hotel room, using the time superficially to put up new curtains, lay plush carpet, install new plumbing, and paint the walls.

Do not store up for yourselves treasures on earth, where moth and rust destroy, and where thieves break in and steal. But store up for yourselves treasures in heaven, where moth and rust do not destroy, and where thieves do not break in and steal. For where your treasure is, there your heart will be also (Matthew 6:19-21).

We Long for a Better Life in a Better Land

Most people who leave one country to live in another place are doing so in search of a better life. Whether we are talking about the first pilgrims to this country hundreds of years ago, or foreign immigrants who stow away in ships in unsanitary conditions, the goal is to find a better life.

It may or may not have happened in your case, but eventually most humans grow weary of life in this world—its shattered dreams, broken promises, painful relationships, and all of its suffering and injustices. Sound familiar? For Christians, the *downs* of this world only serve to intensify our desire for the *ups* of the world to come. With the passing of time, it seems almost inevitable that we will experience a growing desire for our forever home where we will never sigh, cry, or die.

Do you live daily with heaven on your mind? How excited and eager are you to reach the heavenly homeland? Or has the good life of this earth become so attractive that the appeal of heaven is weak or nonexistent? For many today, the growing anti-Christian culture may actually be stirring deep longings for the better land. Could it be that you are feeling the pull of the cross that Paul felt? He wanted to continue serving in the flesh, but he also found the thought of going on to be with Christ "better by far" (Philippians 1:21-24). It is clear in the Scriptures that as the saints of old lived in the midst of hostile conditions, they were not reluctant to let people around them know that they were looking forward to going home.

Come, O Lord! (1 Corinthians 16:22).

Remember those earlier days after you had received the light, when you stood your ground in a great contest in the face of suffering. Sometimes you were publicly exposed to insult and persecution; at other times you stood side by side with those who were so treated. You sympathized with those in prison and joyfully accepted the confiscation of your property, because you knew that you yourselves had better and lasting possessions (Hebrews 10:32-34).

All these people were still living by faith when they died. They did not receive the things promised; they only saw them and welcomed them from a distance. And they admitted that they were aliens and strangers on earth. People who say such things show that they are looking for a country of their own. If they had been thinking of the country they had left, they would have had opportunity to return. Instead, they were longing for a better country— a heavenly one. Therefore God is not ashamed to be called their God, for he has prepared a city for them (Hebrews 11:13-16).

Certainly, we are not saying that Christians are to be totally detached from the affairs of this world or walk about with a morbid obsession for death. Never! But there can and should be an attitude of anticipation as we contemplate the joy of living eternally in an environment where there will be no tempters, no terrorists, no tempests, no termites, no traffic, no travail, no terminal diseases, no threats, no tears, no talebearers, no thorns, no thrombosis, and no tombs. While we sojourn in this foreign region called earth, we are to be filled with Christian hope—a confident expectation of and eagerness for the better land to come. Biblically, for Christians, a departure from this world is not to be viewed as *leaving home* but *going home*.

Max Lucado tells a story about flying home to San Antonio one evening. As the wheels of the plane hit the runway, he said all through the plane you could hear the unfastening of seatbelts. As the voice came over the intercom saying, "Please remain seated with your seatbelt fastened until the plane comes to a complete stop," he said no one was paying attention. People were already out of their seats, opening the overhead compartments, getting their stuff out. Why? Because they were home. Their final destination was not that plane. They wanted to get off that plane, get out, and get home with those they love. He said he didn't see any of the flight attendants having to struggle to pull people out of their seats, with people going, "Wait a minute. I want to stay on the plane for a few more hours. The food is really good. These seats are so comfy, I want to stay." No. They were close to home. And, they wanted to get off that plane to be with their loved ones. They were eager to experience the comforts, joys, sounds, and smells of home. As residents of the land of our first birth, we do long for the homeland of our second birth. Serving here is necessary, but going home is far better (Philippians 1:22, 23).

Think about it like this. When most people talk about what occurs after death, they usually refer to this period as the afterlife. *After life?* From a biblical vantage point, this is incorrect terminology. In fact, we have it just backwards. Our time on this earth is, in one sense, a *before life* experience. The *real life* is yet to come!

We Are Waiting for the Next Main Event

Someone has said, "Waiting is what you do before the main event." The next main event for which we are presently waiting is the Second Coming of Jesus. At that time, the culmination and fulfillment of all redemptive history will occur. Note the following Scriptures that specifically mention "waiting":

> You turned to God from idols to serve the living and true God, and to wait for his Son from heaven, whom he raised from the dead—Jesus, who rescues us from the coming wrath (1 Thessalonians 1:9, 10).

> while we wait for the blessed hope—the glorious appearing of our great God and Savior, Jesus Christ (Titus 2:13).

> But you, dear friends, build yourselves up in your most holy faith and pray in the Holy Spirit. Keep yourselves in God's love as you wait for the mercy of our Lord Jesus Christ to bring you to eternal life (Jude 1:20, 21).

Obviously, the early church was waiting and watching. Has anything changed? Many years ago, in a Jewish village in Eastern Europe, there was a poor crippled man named Yitzhak. The village elders believed strongly in giving everyone dignified work. But there was very little that poor Yitzhak could do, given all of his physical limitations. Therefore, the elders decided to have him sit in the gate of the village from dawn to dusk to wait and watch for the coming of the Messiah. For each day he sat there, ready to shout if the Messiah appeared, he was paid a meager wage. Year after year, Yitzhak watched and waited. One winter, as he shivered in the gate wearing his thin coat, Yitzhak realized that he had not had an increase in pay since he began this watch. So he went to the elders and asked them for a raise. They deliberated, but turned him down saying, "It's true, Yitzhak, that the pay is low, and you have been very faithful. But, you must admit this: 'The work is steady.'" For citizens of heaven residing on earth, the watch goes on and the work of waiting remains steady.

Why Such a Long Wait?

Have you ever wondered why God, seemingly, is taking so long to wrap up His redemptive work and "bring all things in heaven and on earth together under one head, even Christ" (Ephesians 1:10)? Some might ask, "How much longer before the grande finale occurs? When will Jesus come and end the waiting?" Jesus, Himself, answers these questions for us.

"You also must be ready, because the Son of Man will come at an hour when you do not expect him" (Luke 12:40).

"No one knows about that day or hour, not even the angels in heaven, nor the Son, but only the Father. As it was in the days of Noah, so it will be at the coming of the Son of Man. For in the days before the flood, people were eating and drinking, marrying and giving in marriage, up to the day Noah entered the ark; and they knew nothing about what would happen until the flood came and took them all away. That is how it will be at the coming of the Son of Man" (Matthew 24:36-39).

We don't know when Jesus will come back to end our waiting. What we do know is that His coming is nearer now than ever before. There have always been doubters and scoffers who love to say, "You Christians have been waiting two thousand years. Give up and admit that He is not coming."

First of all, you must understand that in the last days scoffers will come, scoffing and following their own evil desires. They will say, "Where is this 'coming' he promised? Ever since our fathers died, everything goes on as it has since the beginning of creation" (2 Peter 3:3, 4).

These mockers forget one important reality. We serve a God who is beyond time. Peter writes

But do not forget this one thing, dear friends: With the Lord a day is like a thousand years, and a thousand years are like a day. The Lord is not slow in keeping his promise, as some understand slowness. He is patient with you, not wanting anyone to perish, but everyone to come to repentance (2 Peter 3:8, 9).

Perhaps you have heard the story about the economist who read the above passage and then talked to God about it. He prayed, "Lord, is it true that a thousand years are just like one minute to you?" The Lord said, "Yes." The economist said, "Well then a million dollars to us must be like one penny to You." And the Lord again said, "Well, yes." The economist then said, "Well,

Lord, will You give me one of Your 'pennies'?" And the Lord said, "I will—just wait a minute."

Too often, we want God's blessings, but not His timing. We forget the importance of the work He is doing within us and through us while we are waiting for the blessed hope. John McArthur writes, "The reason for His delay is not that He's negligent, it's not that He's careless, it's not that He is doing other things. He'll come when His bride for His Son is complete. He'll come when redemption is over."

Waiting Is Not Always Easy

Waiting can be very difficult for us—even painful. We live in the "instant culture." We want answers, service, information, food, and a lot of other things—now! Many of us are not good at waiting.

In checkout lanes at the grocery store, we get agitated. One such woman was fuming as she waited to purchase a new broom, along with some cleaning supplies. She was in one big hurry. With the line not moving fast enough to please her, she was letting everybody around her know that she was not a happy Walmart shopper. Her body language was blaring at full volume. Her loud sighs could be heard. While she counted the service lanes that had been shut down, her blood pressure was going up. When the cashier called for a price check, which delayed her turn at the counter even longer, the woman remarked indignantly, "Well, I'll be lucky to get out of here and home before Christmas!" Picking up on her comment, the clerk replied to the woman, "Don't worry, ma'am. With that wind kicking up out there, and that brand new broom you have there, you'll be home in no time." These reactions to waiting occur all too often. Lines at those fast-food restaurants can take forever. At traffic lights, we expect instant acceleration when the signal turns green. If the driver in front of us is not moving immediately, we are asking, "What shade of green are you waiting for?" No one likes to wait.

Waiting Is to Be a Time for Growth and Renewal

For the believer, this time of waiting is not to be wasted. It is not to be filled with worrying or fretting. Waiting is not to be associated with inactivity, boredom, or complacency. Eugene Peterson's paraphrase of Romans 8:24 is interesting. Describing the time frame that exists between our second birth and the Lord's Second Coming, Peterson renders the verse with these words, "[W]aiting does not diminish us, any more than waiting diminishes a pregnant mother. We are enlarged in the waiting" (*The Message*).

Actually, waiting is closely connected with hope. Hope has been described as creative waiting. It is a powerful force that enables us to see beyond our pain and live with the assurance that in the end everything will be all right.

As stated earlier, Christian hope is a confident expectation—with desire. It views the future with anticipation and assurance that God will keep His promises to us. It stimulates faith and faithfulness. To live in hope is to live with certainty in the power of the future even though you don't yet possess it. Hopeful waiting is a time of high expectancy with life being infused with energy, purpose, and perseverance.

> May the God of hope fill you with all joy and peace as you trust in him, so that you may overflow with hope by the power of the Holy Spirit (Romans 15:13).

> My soul waits for the Lord
> more than watchmen wait for the morning,
> more than watchmen wait for the morning (Psalm 130:6).

> For I am already being poured out like a drink offering, and the time has come for my departure. I have fought the good fight, I have finished the race, I have kept the faith. Now there is in store for me the crown of righteousness, which the Lord, the righteous Judge, will award to me on that day—and not only to me, but also to all who have longed for his appearing (2 Timothy 4:6-8).

Be Patient! Hang On! The Wait Will Be Worth It!

In the very passage where Paul affirms the Christian's heavenly citizenship, he also declares that when we enter the homeland, our earthly bodies will be transformed into glorious bodies like the resurrection body of Jesus. Imagine a perfect body that is suitable to live forever. How can such occur? Paul says that Jesus will do this by the power through which he makes all things subject to Himself. No more will we live in a body of clay—frail and disintegrating! We will be leaving behind these bodies, which Paul refers to as tents. From a tent, you will move into a "building from God, an eternal house in heaven, not built by human hands" (2 Corinthians 5:1). In 1 Corinthians 15, Paul describes our new bodies as being spiritual, glorious, imperishable, and powerful. This is the ultimate makeover to which every faithful believer can look forward. Better days are coming. Hang on. The wait will be worth it.

> But our citizenship is in heaven. And we eagerly await a Savior from there, the Lord Jesus Christ, who, by the power that enables him to bring everything under his control, will transform our lowly bodies so that they will be like his glorious body (Philippians 3:20, 21).

Dear friends, now we are children of God, and what we will be has not yet been made known. But we know that when he appears, we shall be like him, for we shall see him as he is. Everyone who has this hope in him purifies himself, just as he is pure (1 John 3:2, 3).

Not only do we eagerly await our new bodies, but we look forward to the creation of a new heaven and earth in which we shall live and reign with Christ forever.

But the day of the Lord will come like a thief. The heavens will disappear with a roar; the elements will be destroyed by fire, and the earth and everything in it will be laid bare. Since everything will be destroyed in this way, what kind of people ought you to be? You ought to live holy and godly lives as you look forward to the day of God and speed its coming. That day will bring about the destruction of the heavens by fire, and the elements will melt in the heat. But in keeping with his promise we are looking forward to a new heaven and a new earth, the home of righteousness (2 Peter 3:10-13).

In the book of Romans, Paul refers to a time when "the creation itself will be liberated from its bondage to decay and brought into the glorious freedom of the children of God" (Romans 8:21). In Revelation, John reveals more about the "new heaven and earth" that God has promised.

Then I saw a new heaven and a new earth, for the first heaven and the first earth had passed away, and there was no longer any sea. I saw the Holy City, the new Jerusalem, coming down out of heaven from God, prepared as a bride beautifully dressed for her husband. And I heard a loud voice from the throne saying, "Now the dwelling of God is with men, and he will live with them. They will be his people, and God himself will be with them and be their God. He will wipe every tear from their eyes. There will be no more death or mourning or crying or pain, for the old order of things has passed away" (Revelation 21:1-4).

Ten Important Things to Remember and Do While Waiting to Go Home

1 Wait with a sense of the continual presence of God.

Keep your lives free from the love of money and be content with what you have, because God has said, "Never will I leave you; never will I forsake you." So we say with confidence, "The Lord is my helper; I will not be afraid. What can man do to me?" (Hebrews 13:5, 6).

Imagine how different daily life would be if you could live constantly with an awareness of God's presence. This is a discipline that is not easy to practice. It must be desired and cultivated over a period of time. Paul explained to the Athenians that God wants us to seek Him, reach out for Him, find Him, and understand that He is not far from each one of us (Acts 17:27). Augustine said, "Why climb the mountains or go down into the valleys of the world looking for Him who dwells within us?" This means that God is here now and moving through our everyday activities, no matter how trivial they might seem.

To citizens of heaven temporarily residing in the ancient city of Philippi, Paul said, "The Lord is near" (Philippians 4:5). Waiting time can actually be celebrated if we learn to live with a keen awareness of His presence. Begin every day by speaking with God, but don't hang up. Keep silent but vibrant conversations going with your Father all during the day. This is what it means to "pray continually" (1 Thessalonians 5:17). The individual who learns to practice this kind of spiritual awareness will build a courage-building friendship with God that others will not understand or experience. What a wonderful way to live while you wait!

2 Wait with a sense of anticipation and expectancy.

The early church prayed, "Maranatha—Come Lord!" Is this a prayer of the twenty-first-century church? Instead of yearning for His return, many today are yawning. We are to be watching, and we are to stay ready for the coming of Jesus.

> "Be dressed ready for service and keep your lamps burning, like men waiting for their master to return from a wedding banquet, so that when he comes and knocks they can immediately open the door for him. It will be good for those servants whose master finds them watching when he comes. I tell you the truth, he will dress himself to serve, will have them recline at the table and will come and wait on them. It will be good for those servants whose master finds them ready, even if he comes in the second or third watch of the night. But understand this: If the owner of the house had known at what hour the thief was coming, he would not have let his house be broken into. You also must be ready, because the Son of Man will come at an hour when you do not expect him" (Luke 12:35-40).

Back when the telegraph was the fastest means of long-distance communication, there was a story about a young man who applied for a job as a Morse code operator. Answering an ad in the newspaper, he went to the address that was listed. When he arrived, he entered a large, noisy office. In the background a telegraph clacked away. A sign on the receptionist's counter instructed job applicants to fill out a form and wait until they were summoned to enter the inner office. The young man completed his form and sat down with seven other waiting applicants. After a few minutes, the young man stood up, crossed the room to the door of the inner office, and walked right in. Naturally the other applicants perked up, wondering what was going on. Why had this man been so bold? They muttered among themselves that they hadn't heard any summons yet. They took more than a little satisfaction in assuming the young man who went into the office would be reprimanded for his presumption and rejected for the job. Within a few minutes the young man emerged from the inner office escorted by the interviewer, who announced to the other applicants, "Gentlemen, thank you very much for coming, but the job has been filled by this young man." The other applicants began grumbling to each other; then one spoke up, "Wait a minute! I don't understand. He was the last one to come in, and we never even got a chance to be interviewed. Yet he got the job. That's not fair." The employer responded, "All the time you've been sitting here, the telegraph has been ticking out the following message in Morse code: 'If you understand this message, then come right in. The job is yours.' None of you heard it or understood it. This young man did. So the job is his."

There's a good lesson here for us about waiting. The young man got the job because he was not just waiting — all of the other men were waiting — but he was waiting expectantly.

3 Wait with a spirit of contentment—travel light.

As a traveler on your way home, don't get loaded down with a great deal of stuff. None of it is yours anyway, and you can't take it with you when you leave. Ask any funeral director. It all stays behind. Solomon was the richest man of his day. He wrote, "Naked a man comes from his mother's womb, and as he comes, so he departs. He takes nothing from his labor that he can carry in his hand" (Ecclesiastes 5:15). This was true in Solomon's day. It's still true today. So don't get so attached to the stuff of this world.

There is a story about a missionary visiting a leper colony on the island of Molokai many years ago. He was there to encourage the victims of that terrible disease. At one point, he asked if anyone had a favorite song they'd like to sing. When he did, a woman looked at him with the most disfigured face he'd ever seen. She had no ears and no nose. Even her lips were gone. She raised a hand with no fingers and said, "Could we sing, 'Count Your Many Blessings'?" The missionary started the song, but couldn't finish it. He later said, "I'll never sing that song the same way again."

> Since, then, you have been raised with Christ, set your hearts on things above, where Christ is seated at the right hand of God. Set your minds on things above, not on earthly things. For you died, and your life is now hidden with Christ in God. When Christ, who is your life, appears, then you also will appear with him in glory (Colossians 3:1-4).

A man went to a minister for counseling. He was in the midst of financial collapse. "I've lost everything!" he moaned. "I'm so sorry to hear you've lost your faith," said the minister. "No," the man corrected him, "I haven't lost my faith." "Then I'm sad to hear you've lost your character." "I didn't say that," he said, "I still have my character." "Then I'm so sorry to hear you've lost your salvation." "That's not what I said," the man objected. "I haven't lost my salvation." "So you have your faith, your character, and your salvation. Seems to me," said the minister, "you've lost none of the things that really matter."

4 Wait with a firm resolve to keep yourself separated from evil influences that will dilute or destroy your devotion to Christ.

A popular magazine for teenage girls published a statement of purpose. Sadly, this statement reflects the spirit of our age. It read, "This magazine is all about you and everything you want—fashion, beauty, style, travel, people, sensational sex, and a ton of fun." We are living in a culture that constantly sends out the message, "If it feels good, do it!" The world is telling us, "If you want it, you should have it!" The secular mind says, "Why should we allow God or the Bible to tell us how to live our lives?" Many around us believe these lies, and there is a risk that we, too, can be sucked in. To check this risk, Peter urges believers with the following words:

> Dear friends, I urge you, as aliens and strangers in the world, to abstain from sinful desires, which war against your soul. Live such good lives among the pagans that, though they accuse you of doing wrong, they may see your good deeds and glorify God on the day he visits us (1 Peter 2:11, 12).

Note the strong language of this text. There is a fierce war going on and we are in the middle of the crossfire. And get this, the object over which the combatants are fighting is your soul. The phrase "your soul" is a broad term that refers to the new life that you have because of your union with Jesus Christ. The enemy is identified as "sinful desires."

So what are we to do while we are waiting as sojourners who are on our way home? Abstain from sinful desires. We are to have nothing to do with them. Someone said, "Our souls are under construction and God is the foreman of this 'soul project.' Any desire that undermines this project is a desire from which we should run."

> For the grace of God that brings salvation has appeared to all men. It teaches us to say "No" to ungodliness and worldly passions, and to live self-controlled, upright and godly lives in this present age, while we wait for the blessed hope—the glorious appearing of our great God and Savior, Jesus Christ (Titus 2:11-13).

> But the day of the Lord will come like a thief. The heavens will disappear with a roar; the elements will be destroyed by fire, and the earth and everything in it will be laid bare. Since everything will be destroyed in this way, what kind of people ought you to be? You ought to live holy and godly lives as you look forward to the day of God and speed its coming. That day will bring about the destruction of the heavens by fire, and the elements will melt in the heat. But in keeping with his promise we are looking forward to a new heaven and a new earth, the home of righteousness (2 Peter 3:10-13).

5 Wait as a faithful ambassador for Christ in your community.

An ambassador is one who lives in a foreign country as an official representative of his or her native land. We are ambassadors for Christ living in a foreign country we call earth (2 Corinthians 5:17-21). With an understanding of our status, we should make our homes embassies for Christ. An embassy is a building that represents another country within a territory different from itself. Thus when people watch our daily walk and talk, they will be able to see that we are from somewhere else.

A few years ago, my wife and I lived next door to a family who had moved to the United States from India to fulfill a special work assignment. We reached out to them and they graciously reached back. Oh, how they loved their homeland! If we dared to ask anything about India, they were eager to tell us positive things. And as they spoke about their native country, it was obvious that they were missing people, places, and customs back home. They loved to wear the clothing of India. To them it was so attractive and comfortable. As far as food, they much preferred the special dishes of their mother country. Our southern food was okay, but it could not compare with their Indian dishes. On weekends, they frequently entertained in their home other Indian citizens. These occasions were truly reunions and celebrations that had the looks, sounds, and smells of India. The language of choice was one native to India—not English. The music of choice would cause a blindfolded man to think that he had suddenly been immersed into the culture of India. Having lived for a time as their next-door neighbors, we now believe that we were given a tiny sample of what life in the culture of India is like.

This raises a crucial question that we need to address as citizens of heaven. As our daily associates live in proximity to us, are they seeing and sensing the standards of our homeland? While we are waiting for our sojourn on this earth to end, are we clearly reflecting the culture of heaven in our daily practices?

> Devote yourselves to prayer, being watchful and thankful. And pray for us, too, that God may open a door for our message, so that we may proclaim the mystery of Christ, for which I am in chains. Pray that I may proclaim it clearly, as I should. Be wise in the way you act toward outsiders; make the most of every opportunity. Let your conversation be always full of grace, seasoned with salt, so that you may know how to answer everyone (Colossians 4:2-6).

6 Wait with an understanding that you will not be favored by the secular world that surrounds you.

In a culture that is indifferent, or even hostile, to God, don't expect people to gather around you and sing, "For he's a jolly good fellow." Citizens of earth who embrace the views and values of this world cannot be expected to look with favor on believers who reflect the views and values of their heavenly homeland. To many of your daily associates, your beliefs and behaviors may seem radical and ridiculous—too restrictive and burdensome. Some may ridicule, slander, or even oppress. But stand firm. Be courageous and bold. Endure hardship. Never waffle. Don't waiver. Persevere by pondering the good things and the good times that you are soon to enjoy in the heavenly homeland. Just a little longer to wait.

> Praise be to the God and Father of our Lord Jesus Christ! In his great mercy he has given us new birth into a living hope through the resurrection of Jesus Christ from the dead, and into an inheritance that can never perish, spoil or fade—kept in heaven for you, who through faith are shielded by God's power until the coming of the salvation that is ready to be revealed

in the last time. In this you greatly rejoice, though now for a little while you may have had to suffer grief in all kinds of trials (1 Peter 1:3-6).

7 Wait with a confidence that God is at work to transform you into the image of His Son.

We are hard pressed on every side, but not crushed; perplexed, but not in despair; persecuted, but not abandoned; struck down, but not destroyed. We always carry around in our body the death of Jesus, so that the life of Jesus may also be revealed in our body (2 Corinthians 4:8-10).

And we, who with unveiled faces all reflect the Lord's glory, are being transformed into his likeness with ever-increasing glory, which comes from the Lord, who is the Spirit (2 Corinthians 3:18).

The pain of waiting through these, seemingly, endless years of delay serve to teach us vital lessons. The same thing occurred during the lengthy period that God allowed His children to wait and wander in the wilderness prior to entering the Promised Land. God was not as concerned about getting them there *soon* as He was about getting them there *prepared*.

Remember how the Lord your God led you all the way in the desert these forty years; to humble you and to test you in order to know what was in your heart, whether or not you would keep his commands. He humbled you, causing you to hunger and then feeding you with manna, which neither you nor your fathers had known, to teach you that man does not live on bread alone but on every word that comes from the mouth of the Lord. Your clothes did not wear out and your feet did not swell during these forty years (Deuteronomy 8:2-4).

Instead of viewing waiting time with confusion, view it as a time of spiritual construction. God is at work. Two maestros attended a concert to hear a promising young soprano. One commented on the purity of her voice. The other responded, "Yes, but she'll sing better once her heart is broken." You see, there are certain passions only learned by pain. And there are times when God, knowing that, allows us to endure the pain of waiting for the sake of the song He wants us to sing in this foreign land and the homeland to come.

8 Wait with a determination to keep your spiritual gifts deployed in constructive Christian ministry.

A longing for heaven does not mean a loathing for earth. Some have argued that a deep love for heaven will hinder our service on earth and the legitimate responsibilities that we have to it. They feel that a fond vision of heaven could easily become an easy escape from the liabilities of earth.

No! To the contrary, those who have a deep love for heaven will do the most for earth. When the hope of heaven is real, it actually becomes a driving force for more aggressive Christian engagement with the world. C. S. Lewis once said, "It is since Christians have largely ceased to think of the other world that they have become so ineffective in this one." The believer on this earth who sees himself or herself as a member of a colony or outpost of heaven will continually pray and work "for God's will to be done on earth as it is done in heaven." The end result is that more, not less, will be accomplished to serve needy humans in this world.

Jesus' view of His time on this earth must be our view. He said, "As long as it is day, we must do the work of him who sent me. Night is coming, when no one can work. While I am in the world, I am the light of the world" (John 9:4, 5).

> You are the salt of the earth. But if the salt loses its saltiness, how can it be made salty again? It is no longer good for anything, except to be thrown out and trampled by men. You are the light of the world. A city on a hill cannot be hidden. Neither do people light a lamp and put it under a bowl. Instead they put it on its stand, and it gives light to everyone in the house. In the same way, let your light shine before men, that they may see your good deeds and praise your Father in heaven (Matthew 5:13-16).

9 Wait with a fixation on the invisible realities of the heavenly homeland.

> Therefore we do not lose heart. Though outwardly we are wasting away, yet inwardly we are being renewed day by day. For our light and momentary troubles are achieving for us an eternal glory that far outweighs them all. So we fix our eyes not on what is seen, but on what is unseen. For what is seen is temporary, but what is unseen is eternal (2 Corinthians 4:16-18).

While you are waiting, make sure your eyes are fixed in the right place. In the passage above, Paul writes, "So, we fix our eyes not on what is seen, but on what is unseen." Pay attention to that phrase "fix our eyes." The Greek word is *skopeo*, from which we get the words "microscope" and "telescope". The point is that while we are watching and waiting on this earth, we are not to have wandering eyes. We are not to casually look here and there. Instead, we are to fix our eyes, as with a scope, on the invisible and eternal realities of heaven. Unbelievers do not have this ability to see eternal realities (2 Corinthians 2:14; 4:3, 4).

> For, as I have often told you before and now say again even with tears, many live as enemies of the cross of Christ. Their destiny is destruction, their god is their stomach, and their glory is in their shame. Their mind is on earthly things (Philippians 3:18, 19).

Our scope for seeing beyond the mundane and temporal things of this world is faith. With eyes of faith, we are able to see beyond the deceitful treasures of this earth. With eyes of faith, we can see farther than the troubles and pain of this life. In 2 Corinthians 5:7, Paul says, "We live by faith and not by sight." By waiting in faith, you join the distinguished ranks of people like Moses.

> By faith Moses, when he had grown up, refused to be known as the son of Pharaoh's daughter. He chose to be mistreated along with the people of God rather than to enjoy the pleasures of sin for a short time. He regarded disgrace for the sake of Christ as of greater value than the treasures of Egypt, because he was looking ahead to his reward. By faith he left Egypt, not fearing the king's anger; he persevered because he saw him who is invisible (Hebrews 11:24-27).

10 Wait with a valid heavenly passport that will allow you to enter the heavenly homeland.

In order to cross over into the homeland of heaven, you must have a valid passport that has been certified and sealed by the blood of Jesus Christ. The Scriptures are clear.

> Nothing impure will ever enter it, nor will anyone who does what is shameful or deceitful, but only those whose names are written in the Lamb's book of life (Revelation 21:27).

> Blessed are those who wash their robes, that they may have the right to the tree of life and may go through the gates into the city (Revelation 22:14).

Having turned to Jesus Christ in obedient faith and trust, your name is now registered in the Book of Life. Walk with Him daily as the Lord of your life and the Savior of your soul. Never turn back. By doing so, you can live with confidence and security that in the end you will hear Jesus say those wonderful words of welcome, "Come, you who are blessed by my Father; take your inheritance, the kingdom prepared for you since the creation of the world" (Matthew 25:34).

The familiar words of Peter provide a fitting way to close this book. To Christian pilgrims in every century, Peter writes

> Therefore, my brothers, be all the more eager to make your calling and election sure. For if you do these things, you will never fall, and you will receive a rich welcome into the eternal kingdom of our Lord and Savior Jesus Christ (2 Peter 1:10-11).

Ah, home at last!

FOR FURTHER DISCUSSION AND INTERACTION

1   Do you know a saint—perhaps someone who has spent a considerable number of years on this earth as a Christian pilgrim—who would be willing to share his or her perspective on heaven as a going-home experience? Whether the testimony is given in person or taped, this could be a heart-touching and hope-producing experience for the listeners.

2   Ask for comments and examples where people have experienced homesickness in this life. Then, open the discussion for believers to share their homesickness for heaven. As a part of this discussion, it might be insightful to ask members of your group to respond to the question, "Why are we not more homesick for heaven than we are?"

3   Use your imagination. What if Adam and Eve and their descendants had never sinned—even down to this present moment? What would it be like if we were still *at home* in the paradise of Eden and still eating from the tree of life? As you describe life in the original homeland, are you not describing the conditions that we will enjoy in the heavenly homeland? Let your imagination work as you generate fond thoughts of *home*.

4   What should we be doing in local churches to help believers set their minds on things above rather than things below? How has this study helped you gain understanding and perspective on your status as a pilgrim in this world traveling on your way *home*?

5   Many of the old Negro spirituals focused attention on going home. Why was this such a popular theme as songs were composed within that oppressed community? What are the implications of this for us as we compare our conditions *here* with conditions we will experience *there*?

6   Why could it be difficult for many believers in today's world to sing, "This World Is Not My Home?" (Sing or read the words to the song.) Do you see any conditions or circumstances at the present time that may be changing this dynamic? What is going on around us that may make it easier for us to sing this song in a more meaningful way?

7   As followers of Jesus, we are aliens and strangers in this world. Can you cite specific disadvantages, drawbacks, or difficulties that you experience because of your spiritual status and standing in this world?

8   Read Hebrews 10:32-34. Share your thoughts and insights about the conditions that surrounded the first-century believers. Could such

conditions exist in our land? What would change in your life, your family, or your community if there were to be discrimination and oppression shown toward devout followers of Christ?

9 Both Paul and Peter refer to the earthly body as a tent (2 Corinthians 5:1-5; 2 Peter 1:13). Discuss the implications of life in a tent. In the 2 Corinthians passage, our tents are compared to what? Is the idea of a bodily resurrection new to anyone? Discuss this important biblical doctrine. (See John 5:28, 29; 1 Corinthians 15; Philippians 3:20, 21; and 1 John 3:1-3).

10 The last few pages of this chapter list ten things that believers should be remembering and doing while waiting to enter the homeland. Which of these ten is the most meaningful to you at the present time? Explain your answer. Can you identify other helpful waiting exercises that are not included in this list?

11 How has this study changed your view of heaven and your desire to live in the eternal city?

CPSIA information can be obtained
at www.ICGtesting.com
Printed in the USA
FSHW010605111119
63961FS